T0334138

Cambridge Elements ≡

Elements in Earth System Governance
edited by
Frank Biermann
Utrecht University
Aarti Gupta
Wageningen University
Michael Mason
London School of Economics and Political Science (LSE)

ADDRESSING THE GRAND CHALLENGES OF PLANETARY GOVERNANCE

The Future of the Global Political Order

Oran R. Young
University of California, Santa Barbara

CAMBRIDGE
UNIVERSITY PRESS

Shaftesbury Road, Cambridge CB2 8EA, United Kingdom

One Liberty Plaza, 20th Floor, New York, NY 10006, USA

477 Williamstown Road, Port Melbourne, VIC 3207, Australia

314–321, 3rd Floor, Plot 3, Splendor Forum, Jasola District Centre,
New Delhi – 110025, India

103 Penang Road, #05–06/07, Visioncrest Commercial, Singapore 238467

Cambridge University Press is part of Cambridge University Press & Assessment,
a department of the University of Cambridge.

We share the University's mission to contribute to society through the pursuit of
education, learning and research at the highest international levels of excellence.

www.cambridge.org
Information on this title: www.cambridge.org/9781009272476

DOI: 10.1017/9781009272445

First published 2023

A catalogue record for this publication is available from the British Library.

ISBN 978-1-009-27247-6 Paperback
ISSN 2631-7818 (online)
ISSN 2631-780X (print)

Addressing the Grand Challenges of Planetary Governance

The Future of the Global Political Order

Elements in Earth System Governance

DOI: 10.1017/9781009272445
First published online: January 2023

Oran R. Young
University of California, Santa Barbara

Author for correspondence: Oran R. Young, oran.young@gmail.com

Abstract: The world today confronts unprecedented needs for governance having profound implications for human well-being that are difficult – perhaps impossible – to address effectively within the prevailing global political order. This makes it pertinent to ask whether it is necessary to assume that the global order will continue during the foreseeable future to take the form of a state-based society in thinking about options for addressing these challenges. Treating political orders as complex systems and drawing on our understanding of the dynamics of such systems, the author explores the prospects for a critical transition in the prevailing global political order. Individual sections analyze constitutive pressures, systemic forces, tipping elements, the effects of scale, the defining characteristics of potential successors to the current order, and pathways to a new order. In the process, the author seeks to make a more general contribution to our understanding of critical transitions in large political orders.

Keywords: bifurcation, complex system, critical transition, scale, social institution

ISBNs: 9781009272476 (PB), 9781009272445 (OC)
ISSNs: 2631-7818 (online), 2631-780X (print)

Contents

1 Critical Transitions in Political Orders

In my 2021 book on *Grand Challenges of Planetary Governance,* I argue that the world today is confronted with a growing collection of unprecedented needs for governance that have profound implications for human well-being on a global scale but that are difficult – perhaps impossible – to address effectively within the confines of the current global political order (Young 2021). The most familiar example is the climate emergency; maintaining a stable and benign climate system on a human-dominated planet will require fundamental changes in the socioeconomic structures of advanced industrial societies. But this case is not unique. Other prominent examples include the challenge of controlling the spread of infectious diseases that may prove more severe than COVID-19; the difficulty of managing rapidly evolving digital technologies to promote beneficial applications while minimizing a growing array of disruptive uses, and the puzzle of guiding the revolution in biotechnology including the prospect of heritable germline editing. There is every reason to expect that additional needs for governance of this sort will arise in the future.

These challenges have a number of differentiable sources. These include an inability on the part of states to make dependable commitments to contribute to the provision of collective goods (e.g. a benign climate system); a tendency to turn inward, closing national borders in the hope of warding off external threats (e.g. infectious diseases), and the lack of effective means available to authorities to control the actions of those motivated to use sophisticated technologies for antisocial purposes (e.g. cyber terrorism or identify theft). But if my argument is correct, analysts and practitioners concerned about addressing these twenty-first-century challenges of governance must begin to think broadly about the fate of the global political order. What are the prospects that a critical transition will occur in the near future resulting in the emergence of a new order replacing the existing order? What would be the defining features of an alternative order? Would it be easier to address the grand challenges of planetary governance within the new order than within the existing order (Duit and Galaz 2008)? To ask these questions is to launch an enquiry into the forces that control critical transitions in complex systems and, in this case, transformative change in the constitutive features of political orders treated as assemblages of social institutions that guide the activities of human actors in multiple issues areas and provide procedures for arriving at collective choices in these spheres (Jervis 1997; Harrison 2007; Scheffer 2009; Young 2017). An examination of the operation of these forces and their probable consequences with particular reference to political order on a planetary scale is the focus of this Element.[1]

A defining characteristic of political orders ranging from small local orders to the global order is that they are all social constructs. What this means is that they are assemblages of institutional arrangements either created intentionally by human actors seeking to address some consciously delimited domain of human affairs or evolving through recurrent social interactions as distinct and generally stable practices dealing with more-or-less well-defined spheres of human affairs. The elements of such orders do not take the form of natural laws, such as the laws of gravity, that are invariant across both space and time. They are specific to particular times and places and apply to the actions of those active in such settings. This means that political orders are dynamic; they are subject to change as a result of shifts in the capabilities, preferences, and practices of human actors responding to a variety of biophysical and socioeconomic developments. Some of the resultant changes are incremental in nature, as in the case of a court decision setting forth a new interpretation of a specific provision of a national constitution. Such changes do not precipitate transformative shifts in the character of the political order within which they occur. But other changes are more fundamental, producing what those who study complex systems think of as critical transitions or bifurcations in which old orders fall by the wayside and new orders arise (Scheffer 2009).

The current global order shares these features with all other members of the class of political orders. But two factors that make an enquiry into the prospects for a critical transition in this order difficult require recognition at the outset. The prevailing global order is unique in the sense that there is only one political order operating on a planetary scale. We regularly analyze changes occurring within this order. There are lively debates today, for example, regarding shifts in the distribution of power among leading members of the global order and the growing importance of a variety of nonstate actors together with enquiries regarding the political consequences expected to flow from such developments (Kissinger 2014; Allison 2017; Acharaya 2018; Dalio 2021). But the uniqueness of this order makes it impossible to engage in comparative analyses, examining a set of global orders in a search for insights about the determinants of critical transitions at this level.

Treated as a global order, moreover, the current political order has a surprisingly short history. Those of us whose thinking is rooted in the

---

[1] I use the phrase planetary governance in this Element to convey the idea that human societies are embedded in biophysical systems that affect the degree to which societies thrive in significant ways. In this setting, issues of governance include interactions between societies and biophysical systems as well as interactions among human actors.

European experience typically date the inception of the idea of a state-based system to 1648 with the conclusion of the Peace of Westphalia bringing an end to the Thirty Years' War and, in the process, putting in place the defining features of the political order that arose in Europe in the aftermath of this watershed event (Opello and Rosow 2004). As a global political order, however, the prevailing order did not come into existence until the second half of the twentieth century following the onset of wholesale decolonization and the subsequent spread of sovereign states to encompass the landmasses of all the planet's continents other than Antarctica (Bell 2008).[2] In thinking about the future of the current order, therefore, we must reckon with the fact that this unique system has a track record as a global order spanning only a few decades.

Still, there is nothing new about the emergence of large political orders in the sense of orders encompassing extensive spatial areas their inhabitants have typically regarded as the civilized world, though they also involve more-or-less complex interactions with outsiders often lumped together under the rubric of barbarians (Scott 2017; Jones 2021). Prominent examples include large kingdoms, such as Ancient Egypt and China during the Qin and Han Dynasties, centralized empires, such as Imperial Rome, the Mongol Empire, and the Inca Empire, and more complex political orders, such as the Maya Civilization and premodern Europe. There are lively debates about the forces controlling both the rise and the fall of these orders, with proposed explanations pointing to the role of different biophysical and socioeconomic factors and to variations in the importance of internal and external drivers. Explaining the fall of the Western Roman Empire toward the end of the fifth century CE, to take a single prominent example, is a matter of perennial debates among historians who periodically introduce new interpretations regarding the forces that came together to produce this critical transition. There is no doubt that such orders take the form of complex systems in which the interplay of multiple forces makes it difficult to anticipate the occurrence of critical transitions, much less to point to the role of some particular factor as *the* cause of the transition in specific cases (Young 2017). A distinctive feature of all complex systems is the prominence of emergent properties or developments reflecting the impacts of multiple interactive drivers whose individual contributions to the behavior of these systems are impossible to pin down precisely. But one clear conclusion from thinking about these cases is that large political orders are not immune to the operation of tipping elements and the impacts of nonlinear cascades of change that can give rise to critical transitions or what analysts of complex systems

---

[2] Many analysts use the phrase international society in discussing the resultant global order. But because this phrase obscures several features of the prevailing global order, I have chosen to avoid using it in this Element.

often refer to as bifurcations in contrast to oscillations (Lenton et al. 2008; Scheffer 2009). There is no reason to assume that the prevailing global political order constitutes an exception to this observation.

At the level of individual societies, critical transitions in political orders are relatively common (Lebow 2018). As prominent examples, consider the transition associated with the establishment of the United States under the terms of the Constitution negotiated in 1787 and ratified in 1788 to replace the preexisting order articulated in the Articles of Confederation; France's transition from a monarchical to a republican form of order in the decades following the revolution beginning in 1789; the rise of the Soviet order in Russia and surrounding areas following the revolution of 1917; the establishment of new political orders in Germany and Japan following their defeat in World War II, and the rise of the contemporary order in China in the aftermath of the final communist victory in 1949 in a civil war that had raged on and off since the 1920s. The common feature of all these transitions is the occurrence of fundamental change in at least one and often several of the defining or constitutive features of the old order.

Beyond this, differences abound. The American transition took place relatively quickly and in the absence of intense civil strife. On the other hand, it took decades to secure the dominance of a republican order in France. The Soviet order in Russia collapsed after a run of some seven decades. The current order in China has morphed into a system that shows little commitment to the traditional philosophical precepts of communism, though the Communist Party of China retains its position of dominance in China's political order. It is essential to bear in mind the fundamental differences between individual societies and the global order when it comes to thinking about the determinants of critical transitions in political orders. But that said, it is instructive to reflect on the sources of bifurcations in the larger class of political orders as a point of departure for a more intensive effort to think about the future of the prevailing global order treated as a specific case. An analysis of this case also may offer insights regarding the general phenomenon of critical transitions in political orders worthy of investigation in further studies of the dynamics of such orders.

In the substantive sections of this Element, I tackle the questions identified in the opening paragraphs above within the framework of contemporary thinking about the dynamics of complex systems. My argument proceeds as follows. To set the stage, Section 2 provides a brief introduction to current thinking about complex systems. Section 3 directs attention to the defining features of the prevailing global order; it explores developments I call constitutive pressures that have the potential to erode or at least call into question the dominance of one or more of these features. I then move on in Section 4 to examine several developments of a more general nature that I call systemic forces and that may give rise to global changes that have the effect of making the current order obsolete or at least obsolescent. Building on this foundation, I turn in Section 5 to an adaptation of the idea of tipping elements, well known in the literature on Earth system science and complex systems more generally, to the study of critical transitions in the global political order. Taken together, Sections 3–5 provide an assessment of the prospects for the occurrence of transformative change in the existing order.

In the remaining sections, I turn to issues relating to the constitutive features of a potential successor to the existing order. Section 6 drills down on the effects of scale, an issue of sufficient importance in this setting to require special attention in thinking about the future of political order on a planetary scale. Do considerations of scale rule out arrangements at the global level that have proven effective in efforts to address governance challenges in more circum-scribed settings? This sets the stage for an exploration in Section 7 of the constitutive features of a global political order that may succeed the current order in the coming decades. Does the rise of virtual reality provide opportun-ities to introduce workable substitutes for the centralized arrangements typical of smaller societies? Might a successor to the current global order recognize more than one class of members and feature a novel procedure for allocating authority among its members? Finally Section 8 turns to a consideration of pathways to a new global order. Given the character of political orders as complex systems, it is hazardous to offer an explicit forecast regarding the timing of a critical transition leading to the emergence of some distinct succes-sor to the current global order, much less to anticipate the nature of the constitutive features of such a successor. Nevertheless, there is much to be said for engaging in a robust and informed discussion regarding possible trajectories of change in planetary governance. Overall, my goal is to improve our capacity to take advantage of opportunities that arise to address the twenty-first century's grand challenges of planetary governance effectively and, in the process, to contribute to our understanding of the dynamics of political orders more generally.

Before moving on, let me take a moment to situate this assessment in the overarching frame of reference that animates the work of the Earth System Governance community (Biermann 2014). The analysis of critical transitions in political orders brings together this community's concern for architecture and actors on the one hand and its emphasis on transformations on the other hand (Earth System Governance Project 2018). The concern for architecture and actors draws attention to the ways in which institutions shape both the identities and the opportunities available to those who operate within their confines

(Biermann and Kim 2020). But the emphasis on transformations signals an awareness that institutions themselves are social constructs subject to more or less dramatic changes over the course of time. Framing this enquiry as a study of the determinants of critical transitions in political orders signals a sustained interest in processes leading to stability and change in the governance systems human communities devise to guide their collective destinies.

2 Political Orders as Complex Systems

Treating political orders as complex systems provides access to a set of concepts and theoretically grounded propositions that can help us to make progress in understanding the prospects for critical transitions in all political orders, including the prevailing global order. With a few exceptions (Jervis 1997; Harrison 2007; Kavalski 2015), efforts to understand the general features of complex systems have emerged from the work of natural scientists (Levin 1999; Janssen 2002; Johnson 2009; Scheffer 2009). But this does not limit the applicability of this body of work to our efforts to understand the dynamics of political orders.

Like all systems, complex systems involve collections of distinct elements that interact with one another to produce patterned outcomes on a systemic scale (Meadows 2008). Such systems are subject to a variety of feedback processes, including both negative feedback mechanisms serving to constrain forces of change that may disrupt normal operations and positive feedback mechanisms serving to reinforce and in some cases accelerate processes of change once they get underway. Both sorts of mechanisms are operative in most systems, and the relative importance of these mechanisms is apt to change over the course of time. As a proper subset of the broader class of systems, however, complex systems share a number of distinctive features that are of particular interest to those concerned with the dynamics of political orders.

2.1 Telecoupling

To begin with, complex systems are subject to what systems analysts have come to regard as telecoupling (Liu et al. 2013, 2015; Kapsar et al. 2019). The essence of telecoupling is the existence of linkages between or among elements of a system that appear on the surface to be distant or unrelated but that turn out to be of great importance. In the Earth's climate system, for example, melting occurring on the Greenland icecap has the effect of raising global sea levels producing more or less dramatic impacts on small islands located in the South Pacific. Similarly, political disturbances occurring in Syria and other parts of the Middle East trigger cross-border flows of migrants that generate domestic crises in European countries like Germany and Greece when migrants seek to enter these countries as refugees. Telecoupling is a variable; the resultant links may be loose or tight and become looser or tighter over the course of time. As telecoupling becomes tighter, as appears to be happening in the global political order today, it becomes increasingly important to watch for important links that may seem anything but self-evident until we uncover the mechanisms that give rise to them.

2.2 Nonlinear Change

A related feature of complex systems is the prominence of nonlinear and sometimes exponential processes of change. We are used to thinking about systemic changes that occur gradually or incrementally over the course of time. We anticipate that glaciers will melt slowly over decades or centuries; we expect public opinion regarding matters of current interest to shift gradually over time. But in complex systems, this is not uniformly the case. Although most glaciers do melt slowly, specific glaciers may reach thresholds leading to sudden dramatic collapses. While public opinion does shift gradually under some circumstances, there are also cases in which sharp transitions occur over remarkably short periods of time. Often, such nonlinear developments occur once a threshold or what those who study complex systems often call a tipping point is passed (Gladwell 2002). Think of the rapid and dramatic consolidation of American public opinion regarding the participation of the United States in World War II following the Japanese attack on Pearl Harbor on December 7, 1941, or the coalescence of public opinion in Finland and Sweden regarding membership in NATO in the wake to the Russian invasion of Ukraine on February 24, 2022. This makes the study of the nature of tipping elements in general and the character of trigger mechanisms more specifically a matter of intense interest to those seeking to understand the dynamics of complex systems.

2.3 Oscillations and Bifurcations

This leads as well to an emphasis on the distinction between what analysts call systemic oscillations and bifurcations (Lenton et al. 2008). Oscillations involve fluctuations in the behavior of a system whose magnitude and timing are controlled by the operation of negative feedback mechanisms. Seasonal fluctuations in the Earth's climate system provide a prominent case in point. Much modern thinking in the field of macroeconomics centers on efforts to construct feedback mechanisms that employ a range of monetary and fiscal policies designed to control the fluctuations associated with business cycles. Bifurcations, by contrast, occur when systems break through the boundaries imposed by negative feedback mechanisms, shifting from an initial state to some wholly different state or from what some analysts describe as one basin of attraction to another (Scheffer et al. 2012; van der Leeuw and Folke 2021). This is the focus of the recent literature exploring what analysts call planetary boundaries (Rockström et al. 2009; Steffen et al. 2015). Critical transitions are, in effect, bifurcations, and I will use both terms in analyzing the future of the global political order. Clearly, a prominent focus of attention in this context involves the boundaries separating situations subject to oscillations in contrast to bifurcations together with trigger mechanisms that can push systems across such boundaries. An important observation in this context is that once a threshold or tipping point is reached, a relatively modest trigger mechanism may suffice to catalyze a cascade of developments leading to a critical transition (Gladwell 2002).

2.4 Emergent Properties

It should come as no surprise, under the circumstances, that complex systems typically exhibit what analysts describe as emergent properties (O'Connor 2020). The key insight here is that outcomes emerging from interactions among the elements of complex systems involve the impacts of so many variables that it is generally impossible to predict their nature and timing precisely, much less to attribute specific outcomes to the impacts of simple causal mechanisms. The development of increasingly sophisticated models makes it possible to analyze the dynamics of some complex systems with greater precision. This is why we are now able to produce weather forecasts that do a reasonably good job of predicting weather conditions unfolding over a few days rather than over just a few hours (Coiffier 2012). Nevertheless, emergent properties make it extremely difficult to anticipate the behavior of really complex systems with any precision. A prominent case in point involves the difficulties of projecting the likely trajectory of climate change on a global scale even over the course of the next few years. A moment's thought will suffice to make it clear that this difficulty is front and center with regard to efforts to anticipate the trajectory of changes in political orders. This is why most observers were taken by surprise by the onset of the French Revolution in 1789 and the collapse of the Soviet Union in 1991, though they were aware of destabilizing forces that had been present in these political orders for some time. The upshot is that surprise is a common feature of our efforts to understand the behavior of complex systems. We may endeavor to limit the scope for surprise in thinking about the dynamics of such systems. But we must also learn to live with relatively high levels of uncertainty about matters like the timing and nature of critical transitions in large political orders.

With this analytic framework in hand, we can return to the central focus of this Element. What are the prospects for the occurrence of a critical transition in the global political order treated as a complex system? What forces might trigger a bifurcation in this realm? In the event that a bifurcation does occur, what form might an alternative order take? Before tackling these questions, however, let me pause to comment on a tension arising from the treatment of political orders as complex systems. This analytical framework offers a way forward for those interested in enhancing our understanding of the dynamics of political orders. But many analysts and policymakers take an interest in this subject, in part at least, because they want to improve our ability to address contemporary needs for governance. As I have noted, both the timing and the results of critical transitions are difficult to anticipate clearly; surprises are common in the world of complex systems. Those who are not content simply to augment our understanding of the dynamics of political orders will find this situation perplexing. It makes it difficult to distill from the analysis clear policy recommendations. The resultant tension is real. But it is important not to exaggerate its importance. It is naive to think that we can make accurate predictions regarding the probable consequences of policy initiatives under any circumstances (Harrison 2007). At the same time, there is much to be said for improving our understanding of the roles of telecoupling, nonlinear changes, and emergent properties in complex systems as a way to avoid naive expect-ations about the relative merits of various options for responding to specific needs for governance under real-world conditions.

3 Constitutive Pressures

One way to engage in systematic thinking about the prospects for a critical transition in the prevailing global political order is to focus on the constitutive features of this order one at a time, asking in each case about the resilience of the feature or, in other words, its capacity to adapt to emerging challenges without undergoing fundamental change (Gunderson and Holling 2002; Folke 2006). Proceeding in this way, I direct attention to matters of membership, authority, and obligation, starting with conventional formulations of these features and considering developments leading to significant changes in these institutional arrangements over time. The traditional view of membership centers on the requirements a social entity must fulfill to be recognized as a state and conse-quently eligible to be treated as a member of the global order. Authority then refers to the principle that member states have the right to exercise control over matters taking place within their jurisdictional boundaries. Obligation, on this account, has to do with interactions among the members of the global order. In its simplest form, this feature of the current global order asserts that states cannot be bound by obligations they do not accept on a voluntary basis.

Like other political orders, the prevailing global order is dynamic. It evolves in response to a variety of forces developing over time and often interacting with one another to produce effects that are systemic in character. Some of these effects, such as the emergence of new states that are accepted as members of the global order, are easy to accommodate without altering the constitutive foundations of this system. Others, such as shifts in the distribution of power among the members of the current order, have consequences that are important but not because they change the character of the system (Kissinger 2014). Still others, such as the emergence of many new issues (e.g. international air travel, commercial shipping on a large scale, the rise of the Internet), generate distinct needs for governance. But so long as states take the lead in responding to them through the creation of (increasingly complex) international regimes, the treatment of these issues does not raise serious questions about the nature of the current order.

Other developments, by contrast, lead to changes that have the potential to shift the character of the current political order in more or less fundamental ways. Among the most important of these developments are the growing importance of various types of nonstate actors, the increasing frequency of efforts to accord some of these actors the authority to make decisions without reference to the preferences of individual states, and the emergence of a denser web of relationships that entangle states and make it difficult for them to exercise the freedom to make their own decisions about specific issues. Some analysts, especially those who belong to the English School of thinking about international relations and who have articulated the idea of solidarism, make the case that these developments taken together have transformed the character of the global order or, in any case, are in the process of doing so (Linklater and Suganami 2006; Hurrell 2007). How persuasive is this line of thinking? Do we need to restructure our understanding of the prevailing order as a result?

3.1 Membership

The conventional view is that membership in the global order is reserved for states treated as social units that are spatially delimited, include well-defined human populations, have governments capable of making and implementing collective choices applicable to all those subject to their jurisdiction, and are recognized by others as fulfilling these conditions (Bull 1977).[3] One famous definition of statehood attributed to Max Weber asserts that states have governments possessing a monopoly on the legitimate use of coercive force regarding events occurring within the confines of their jurisdiction (Weber 1930). But the critical requirement for statehood centers on the existence of a governance system that is capable of steering the course of events involving interactions among an identifiable group of subjects located within a spatially delimited area. This leaves room for great variation within the universe of states. For example, we commonly speak of nation-states, multicultural states, microstates, city states, coastal states, small-island states, petro-states, failed states, and so forth.

The decades since the close of World War II have witnessed both a sharp rise in the number of members of the global political order and an expansion of the collection of states to encompass all the land masses of the planet, with the notable exception of Antarctica. In 1945, at the close of the World War II, it was possible to identify some fifty to sixty states. The United Nations included fifty-one founding members, with a strong representation of states located in Europe and the Americas. Today, the organization has 193 members, including 54 African states, 38 small-island developing states, and 15 former Soviet Republics that became independent states following the dissolution of the Soviet Union at the end of 1991 (see Box 1). The majority of the states belonging to the United Nations in 2022 did not exist as independent states at the close of World War II. Further developments are possible. Individual states may amalgamate to form unified successor states or fragment to produce two or more successor states; some small-island states may literally disappear as a consequence of sea level rise. But the membership of the global order is now planetary in scope. There is no prospect of a recurrence of the dramatic growth in the number of independent states that marked the final decades of the twentieth century.

From one perspective, these observations point to the triumph of the state-based global order. What began several centuries ago as a European invention designed to address an intractable problem arising in the European order of the late middle ages has evolved into a global political order. The membership has expanded to encompass all the Earth's land masses; states have extended their jurisdiction to include both extensive marine areas adjacent to their coasts and superjacent airspace.

---

[3] There is no universally accepted formula specifying the attributes of statehood. Perhaps the most authoritative formulation occurs in Art. 1 of the 1933 Montevideo Convention on the Rights and Duties of States specifying that a state must possess a permanent population, defined territorial boundaries, a government, and the ability to enter into agreements with other states – oas.org/juridico/english/treaties/a-40.html.

With the exception of a few ambiguous and controversial cases, such as Kosovo, North Korea, Palestine, and South-West Somalia, all states have applied for and been granted membership in the United Nations. This makes it possible to monitor developments relating to membership in the current global political order by tracking changes in the membership of the United Nations. As Figure 1 shows, the United Nations started with 51 members at the time of its founding in 1945 and has grown over time to a current total of 193 members.[4] Growth in membership was especially rapid during the period starting in about 1960 and running through the early 1990s but has leveled off in recent years. Decolonization accounts for the lion's share of the United Nations' expanded membership, though high-profile events like the breakup of the Soviet Union resulting in the establishment of the Russian Federation together with fifteen additional successor states are notable as well.

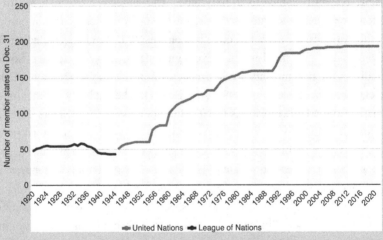

Figure 1 United Nations membership
Source: © Statista 2022, www.statista.com/statistics/1057158/number-lon-un-member-states-since-1920/.

The majority of the current members of the state-based system did not exist as recognized states in 1945 at the close of World War II. Because states now cover all the planet's landmasses with the exception of Antarctica, it is unlikely that there will be major changes in the membership of the society of states during the foreseeable future. Still, some changes in

---

4 As a concession to the Soviet Union, Byelorussia and Ukraine were accepted as separate members of the UN in 1945.

membership over time are to be expected due to political developments such as the fragmentation of existing states or the unification of two or more current states or as a result of biophysical forces like the destruction of existing states due to the impacts climate change.

Yet it would be a mistake to infer from these developments that the state-based system is now so solidly entrenched that it is immune to the forces of change. With regard to the matter of membership, it is useful to consider both questions pertaining to social units currently accepted as states and questions about social units that have the capacity to influence the course of events on a global scale despite the fact that they do not meet the qualifications for acceptance as states.

Although the roster of states currently includes almost 200 members, many of these states suffer from internal turmoil that raises questions about the viability of their governance systems; some may disappear entirely during the foreseeable future. There are several dozen micro-states with a population of less than a million people. Some of these states (e.g. Iceland) perform well as states; others are more notional and have difficulty functioning effectively as members of the state-based system. Many larger states are plagued with internal problems that impede efforts to maintain or put in place effective governance systems. In extreme cases, such as Somalia and Yemen today, it is common to refer to these states as failed states. This is not to say that this is a permanent condition in any given case. But protracted civil strife undermines the ability of a significant number of social units currently accepted as members of the global order to function as states.

Beyond this lies the prospect that some current states will simply disappear as a consequence of the onset of climate change. Some small-island states, for example, are already considering the prospect that they will need to abandon their territory as a result of the impact of sea level rise. Even some coastal states like Bangladesh may find their ability to function effectively as states severely impaired by the impacts of climate change. Thus, there is no basis for assuming that the membership of the global order is settled and unlikely to change in the future. On the contrary, membership in this political order is fluid. More or less substantial changes in membership will occur over time.

At the same time, recent decades have witnessed the rise of a range of nonstate actors that can and do exercise influence on a global scale in ways that are difficult or impossible for states to control (Hall and Biersteker 2002). Some of these actors play roles that exceed the roles that many states play. To explore the significance of this development, it is helpful to divide the category of nonstate actors into corporate actors such as transnational corporations (TNCs) and civil society organizations (CSOs) including what are often referred to as nongovernmental organizations (NGOs).

The largest TNCs have revenue streams that exceed the GDPs of all but the largest states. With the globalization of the world economy, corporations have become the linchpins of an increasingly complex planetary economic system. Legally, each TNC is incorporated under the laws of some particular state. In principle, this means they are subject to control on the part of their home states. But as they have expanded their operations to reach all corners of the Earth system, these actors have become adept at escaping the regulatory authority of individual states. We are witnessing today a struggle between states and TNCs to determine whether states can (re)assert effective control over the activities of these nonstate actors. The efforts of China to clip the wings of Chinese corporations like Alibaba, Baidu, and Tencent are particularly striking in this regard. So are the impacts on transnational economic relationships resulting from the Ukraine crisis. These are messy processes; the jury is out regarding the eventual balance of power between states and corporate nonstate actors. But there is no doubt that corporate nonstate actors have become powerful players on the global stage in recent decades, exercising influence that states find it difficult if not impossible to control on a day-to-day basis.

CSOs, too, are normally rooted in the political systems of individual states that can, at least in principle, exercise control over their activities. But these actors also have expanded the scope of their activities to become influential players in a number of issue areas, including human rights (e.g. Amnesty International), human health (e.g. the Gates Foundation), food security (e.g. the Rockefeller Foundation), and environmental protection (e.g. the Worldwide Fund for Nature). In a showdown, would states be able to exercise effective control over the activities of these nonstate actors? It is difficult to answer this question in any straightforward way. But there is little doubt that the stage of planetary governance is populated increasingly by a range of nonstate actors capable of operating autonomously rather than acting as extensions of the states in which they are nominally rooted.

Another development of considerable interest involves the rise of transnational social movements and what some observers have characterized as global action networks or GANs (Smith et al. 1997; Kaldor 2003; Waddell and Khagram 2007). GANs are loosely organized and lightly administered associations that typically direct attention to specific issues, such as the Global Alliance for Vaccines and Immunization, the Access Initiative, or Transparency International. GANs are not about to displace states as the principal actors in world affairs. Nevertheless, networks of this sort are proliferating and becoming forces of some significance in a growing range of issue areas. What makes them particularly interesting in this assessment is that they are structured as loosely controlled networks; they exercise influence while making no effort to present themselves as organized actors that could become competitors to states as sources of authority.

It is not surprising, under the circumstances, that we are witnessing a rapid rise in interest in what have become known as public–private partnerships (PPPs) (Andonova 2017). It is not easy to launch a PPP that is capable of playing an effective role in addressing some specific issue or issue domain in the realm of Earth system governance. Many partnerships initiated with great expectations have produced disappointing results. But the important point in terms of this discussion is the growing realization that coming to terms with a range of planetary concerns will require collaboration between states and nonstate actors treated as partners rather than as players subordinated to the regulatory control of one or more states. The result is that while membership in the global political order is still open only to social units that qualify as states, we operate now in a world populated by several types of nonstate actors and loosely structured networks that make a difference in efforts to address the rising challenges of planetary governance.

3.2 Authority

As a general principle, states regarded as members of the prevailing order are treated as having the authority to deal as they see fit with all activities taking place within the confines of their jurisdictional boundaries. They may establish criteria for citizenship, determine the scope of the rights accorded to citizens and the duties imposed on them, establish their own domestic political systems, regulate economic activities occurring within their boundaries, and establish rules governing all movements of people across their borders. In a world of self-contained units focusing on their own affairs and engaging in only limited interactions with outsiders, the concept of internal sovereignty seems relatively straightforward. States are self-contained units expected to handle their own affairs in the absence of interference on the part of outsiders. In today's more complex world, however, this seemingly simple feature of the global order is subject to increasingly serious assault both in normative terms and in empirical or positive terms.

Some of the challenges to internal sovereignty are normative or prescriptive. A first step in this direction is embedded in the provisions of the Charter of the United Nations. While Article 2(7) states that "[n]othing in the present Charter shall authorize the United Nations to intervene in matters that are essentially within the domestic jurisdiction of any state," it also asserts that "this principle shall not prejudice the application of enforcement measures under Chapter VII" (United Nations 1945). In other words, the principle of internal sovereignty is reaffirmed, but states are not allowed to engage in activities within their domestic jurisdiction leading to what Chapter VII calls "threats to the peace, breaches of the peace, and acts of aggression" (United Nations 1945). The willingness of the permanent members of the Security Council to exercise their right to veto measures they dislike has had the effect of limiting the significance of this restriction on internal sovereignty in practice. The result, in the minds of many, is a system that amounts to a continuation of great-power politics by another name. Still, the provisions of Chapter VII constitute a first step toward recognition of the idea that internal sovereignty is not indivisible.

More recently, members of the prevailing order have begun to articulate other principles that can be deployed to justify interventions in the domestic affairs of others (see Box 2). Perhaps the most significant case focuses on efforts to combat alleged violations of human rights as articulated in authoritative documents such as the 1948 Universal Declaration of Human Rights (UDHR 1948) and formalized in international legally binding instruments adopted during the 1960s. Specific cases of humanitarian intervention justified as efforts to safeguard human rights are always contentious. But the point is that growing support for the legitimacy of the principle of humanitarian intervention

---

Box 2 Humanitarian Intervention

We commonly associate the idea of internal sovereignty with the seventeenth-century Peace of Westphalia that established the principle that outsiders have no authority to interfere in the domestic affairs of independent states, particularly when it comes to matters of religion. Generalized to all issues and to all states, the 1933 Montevideo Convention on the Rights and Duties of States asserts in Art. 8 that "No state has the right to intervene in the internal or external affairs of another." Art. 2(7) of the United Nations Charter adopted in 1945 extends this principle, stating that "Nothing contained in the present Charter shall authorize the United Nations to intervene in matters that are essentially within the domestic jurisdiction of any state." Formulated in these terms, the principle of internal sovereignty seems absolute. Interpreted literally, it suggests that outsiders have no right to seek to impose limitations on the actions of states within their own jurisdictions, regardless of the extent to which they believe these actions violate overarching moral or ethical principles.

Yet there is another stream of thinking that appears to run counter to this view and that many have argued provides a basis for humanitarian intervention in the domestic affairs of states. Nowhere is this more clear than in the provisions of the Universal Declaration of Human Rights adopted by the United Nations General Assembly in 1948. Laying out a suite of critical human rights, the Universal Declaration states that "every organ of society" shall strive to secure the "universal and effective recognition and observance of these rights." Prominent examples include the assertions that "Everyone has the right to freedom of thought, conscience and religion" (Art. 18) and that "Everyone has the right to freedom of opinion and expression" (Art. 19).

There is no simple way to reconcile these discordant principles. Some states, such as the Peoples Republic of China, have deployed the principle of domestic sovereignty to reject outside interference regarding the treatment of minorities residing in areas like Tibet and Xinjiang. Others, such as the United States, have wielded principles of human rights to justify humanitarian intervention in the domestic affairs of others, while rejecting the judgments of outsiders regarding domestic issues of human rights regarding the status of Blacks and Native Americans. Still others seem willing to consider formulations designed to adjust the principle of internal sovereignty in a way that confirms basic human rights and that could serve as a justification for at least some forms of humanitarian intervention.

This is a critical fault line in the prevailing global order. It is difficult to see any prospect of a clearcut resolution of differences focused on the theme of humanitarian intervention during the foreseeable future.

constitutes a development that is at odds with conventional interpretations of the idea of internal sovereignty. Similar developments in other areas are also worth noting. In recent years, for example, powerful states have begun to argue that it is acceptable to intervene with or without the approval of the United Nations in the domestic affairs of states that harbor terrorist groups such as al-Qaeda. It is difficult to forecast future developments regarding normative limitations on the exercise of internal sovereignty. Will the disruptive consequences arising from the onset of climate change, for example, emerge as a justification for interventions in the domestic affairs of states that are unwilling to take prompt and effective steps to curb emissions of greenhouse gases occurring within their jurisdiction? But it is clear that we have moved beyond earlier assertions that nothing could justify actions running counter to the principle of internal sovereignty (Lyons and Mastanduno 1995).

Turning from normative to empirical considerations, it is obvious that de facto interventions on the part of powerful states in the domestic affairs of others are commonplace. The principle of internal sovereignty is meant to serve as a deterrent to such interventions by driving up the political costs to those who launch them. This is why intervenors often seek the approval of others and especially the approval of the United Nations in an effort to justify their actions. The creation in 2011 of the United Nations Support Mission in Libya is a prominent example. At the same time, as the cases of the 2003 intervention in Iraq by the United States and its supporters and Russia's 2022 military actions in Ukraine make clear, there is nothing unusual about great-power intervention, including armed intervention, in the domestic affairs of lesser states that have incurred the displeasure of powerful states like the United States or Russia.

What is new in this realm is the dramatic growth in the range and severity of cyber interventions in the domestic affairs of states. Sometimes, this is the work of private rogue actors using ransomware to extort payments from their victims or simply deploying malware to demonstrate their capacity to disrupt everyday life in modern societies. But in many cases, digital intervention is the work of government agents or agencies using malware to disrupt the governance systems of rival states in the interests of enhancing their ability to exercise power in their interactions with other members of the global political order (Kaplan 2016; Segal 2016; Perlroth 2020). The dramatic interventions of Russia aimed at skewing the operation of the America electoral system constitute a particularly prominent but by no means unparalleled example. There is little doubt that interventions of this sort are destined to increase in frequency, variety, and severity during the coming years (Klimburg 2017; Perlroth 2020).

Does this mean that the principle of internal sovereignty is on the way out on a global scale? Not necessarily. Violations of constitutive provisions of political orders occur in all cases, and the current global order is no exception. So, it would be inappropriate to jump to dramatic conclusions regarding the resilience of this feature of the prevailing order. The critical issue is whether it will be possible to find a way to adapt to the normative and empirical challenges described in the preceding paragraphs in such a way that the authority of states to deal with their domestic affairs remains largely intact. I will have more to say about this matter in the discussion of systemic forces in the next section. For now, it will suffice to observe that this issue constitutes a central concern in any effort to arrive at convincing answers to the questions articulated at the beginning of this Element.

3.3 Obligation

Many analysts have observed that the state-based system can be thought of as an anarchical society (Bull 1977). It is a society rather than simply a system of interacting elements because the constitutive features of the global order take the form of social institutions that define membership and guide the activities of the members of this society. The principle that only states are eligible to become members of the global order, for example, is not a fact of life. It is an institutionalized arrangement accepted by the member states and acknowledged by others that are actors in their own right but not regarded as members of this political order. At the same time, the state-based system is anarchical in the sense that there is no overarching body with the authority to make decisions that are binding regarding the behavior of its members and the capacity to persuade or compel member states to comply with these decisions. Sometimes referred to as the principle of external sovereignty, this feature of the current order ensures that states are obligated to act in accordance with collective choices only in those cases where they have given their consent voluntarily.

The principle of external sovereignty is an entrenched feature of the current order. The operation of this principle explains why it is so difficult to make progress in developing collective responses to priority concerns like the onset of climate change or the diffusion of infectious diseases such as COVID-19. Where collective choices require consent on the part of all participants in the process, there is a tendency for outcomes to take the form of no agreement or agreement on the lowest common denominator at best. This does not preclude the formation of negotiating blocs and the occurrence of processes of institutional bargaining of the sort often referred to as logrolling in studies of legislative politics in domestic systems (Sebenius 1984; Tsebelis 2003). Nevertheless, voluntary consent on the part of all participants is a high bar to clear. It explains why efforts to address major global issues are often agonizingly slow and eventuate in agreements on arrangements that are not legally binding as in the case of the Nationally Determined Contributions that constitute a prominent innovation in the 2015 Paris Climate Agreement.

Still, it would be a mistake to ignore a number of developments that have the effect of imposing limits on the principle of external sovereignty. Members of the United Nations, for example, acknowledge the authority of the Security Council to make binding decisions relating to "threats to the peace, breaches of the peace, and acts of aggression" (United Nations 1945). The operation of the veto on the part of one or more of the permanent members of the council has limited the practical significance of this arrangement. But it is a major departure from business as usual that could become increasingly important over time. Nor is this the only example of the emergence of limitations on the principle of external sovereignty (Squatrito et al. 2018). Those states that have accepted the compulsory jurisdiction of the International Court of Justice acknowledge the authority of the court to make rulings on specific cases to which they are a party without seeking their consent on a case-by-case basis. States that have accepted the 1998 Rome Statute creating the International Criminal Court acknowledge the authority of the court to try and convict individuals including political leaders accused of committing crimes against humanity without seeking their consent in each case. For its part, the World Trade Organization operates a Dispute Settlement Mechanism whose authority member states accept by virtue of their acceptance of the legally binding agreement establishing the organization. None of these developments comes close to creating an arrangement deserving to be thought of as a world government. Great powers, in particular, can and do ignore all these restrictions on their external sovereignty on a regular basis. Even so, they are sufficiently significant to make it clear that we need to proceed with care in thinking about the state-based system as an anarchical society.

Beyond this lies the realm of customary international law. Even in an anarchical society, some practices arise and acquire the status of prescriptive obligations, despite the fact that they are not articulated in legally binding instruments and have not been acknowledged formally by the members of the political order. For example, the United States has refused to ratify the 1982 UN Convention on the Law of the Sea, but it takes the view that most of the content of the modern law of the sea has acquired the status of customary international law binding on the members of the global order. There are obvious limitations on the extent to which customary practices can make up for deficits in formal obligations in an anarchical society. Still, many traditional societies have made do with the evolution of what is generally called common law in domestic political orders. A critical challenge on a planetary scale has to do with whether the pace of the evolution of customary international law can keep up with the rise of increasingly important needs for governance in the twenty-first century (Galaz 2014).

Overall, there is no compelling reason at this stage to alter our characterization of the state-based system as an anarchical society. But it is equally important to avoid simplistic interpretations regarding the meaning of this condition in practice. There is a good deal of experience with what are often called stateless societies operating at various levels. Studies of small orders have demonstrated that stateless societies can find effective ways to address needs for governance under a variety of conditions (Graeber and Wengrow 2021). The question here is whether these findings suggest that these processes can work at the level of planetary governance, especially in responding to an array of needs for governance that threaten to precipitate critical transitions if they are not attended to promptly and effectively.

What can we conclude from this discussion of constitutive pressures? Without doubt, the prevailing global order is dynamic. Many of the developments discussed in this section have important implications for the treatment of needs for governance arising in today's world; significant shifts will continue to unfold during the foreseeable future. Still, it would be difficult to make a convincing case for the proposition that the global political order has crossed some threshold requiring us to abandon our description of it as a state-based society, replacing this characterization with some new understanding of the prevailing global political order. There is no basis for optimism regarding the capacity of the existing order to evolve on a piecemeal basis during the near future allowing it to produce effective responses to the twenty-first century's grand challenges of planetary governance. But this observation does not justify the conclusion that the prevailing order is no longer a state-based society.

4 Systemic Forces

Another way to think about the prospects for a critical transition in the global political order is to focus on what I call systemic forces or, in other words, large and increasingly powerful developments leading to changes that threaten to erode or overwhelm this order as we have known it in recent times. I began this enquiry in the concluding chapter of my 2021 book on the *Grand Challenges of Planetary Governance* (Young 2021). Here, I sharpen and extend the analysis by exploring three separate themes: tightened telecoupling, the digital revolution, and the emergence of unprecedented needs for governance. Telecoupling is a matter of the development of linkages on a planetary scale that make it difficult for states to exercise effective control over events occurring within their own jurisdiction. The digital revolution giving rise to virtual reality in contrast to physical or material reality poses increasingly fundamental threats to the viability of a political order in which membership is limited to social units defined in territorial or spatial terms. As indicated at the outset, the emergence of what I call grand challenges refers to the rise of a collection of distinct and unprecedented needs for governance on a planetary scale that are difficult – perhaps impossible – to address within the confines of the prevailing order.

4.1 Tightened Telecoupling

A familiar perspective on international relations employs a metaphor in which hard-shelled units thought of as billiard balls ricochet off one another on a regular basis without forming lasting attachments. As applied to the global order, this metaphor implies that states are in full control of their internal affairs and that their interactions with one another do not eventuate in major internal changes or in constraints that restrict their freedom to act independently in the future. Whatever the merits of this metaphor as applied to other political orders, however, it is not helpful as a point of departure for thinking about the prevailing global order. We live in an increasingly complex system in which cascades of developments that individual states are incapable of anticipating, much less controlling effectively, are common, and teleconnections generate situations in which events unfolding in particular parts of the system produce surprising and sometimes counterintuitive impacts at distant locations. What this means is that while states may retain the authority in principle to deal with matters occurring within the limits of their jurisdiction, hyper-connectivity is creating a situation in which their capacity to exercise control over such matters in practice is on the decline.

The burgeoning literature on globalization, especially in the realms of economics and political economy, constitutes one major stream of thinking regarding this systemic force (Keohane and Nye 1977; Cox 1987; Stiglitz 2003; Sachs 2020). The focus here is on the dramatic growth in international trade and foreign direct investment occurring during the decades following World War II. We now have a global economy in which numerous transnational corporations have become influential players in their own right, supply chains have grown longer and more complex, 90 percent of everything moves by ship from one country to another, and sophisticated financial practices allow powerful players to escape the tax regimes and regulatory policies of their home states. The result, according to those who focus on the impacts of globalization, is a world in which states find themselves increasingly entangled in a web of economic relationships that have far-reaching consequences for all those living within their jurisdictions but that they are unable to control effectively.

As some acute observers have noted, however, it is easy to get carried away by this line of thinking (Rodrik 2012). Economic linkages among the major states rose to high levels during the final decades of the nineteenth century and the early years of the twentieth century. But this did not prevent the outbreak of World War I, leading not only to a protracted war in which states were the principal protagonists but also to a severe disruption of the international economic system setting in motion developments leading to the onset of the Great Depression in the late 1920s and, less directly, to World War II. Even today, there are clear indications that major states retain the capacity to rein in the activities of economic actors when the choose to do so. Interesting developments in this regard include the intensification of friction between China and the United States producing incentives for major economic players to shorten supply chains, the impacts of the COVID-19 pandemic, and the actions of the Chinese leadership driven by a desire to assert control over the activities of large corporate players like Alibaba, Baidu, and Tencent. The economic fallout from the war in Ukraine will add to the complexity of this picture. How these developments will play out during the coming years is far from clear; the balance of power between states and major corporations is remarkably fluid at this juncture. But it would be inappropriate to take it for granted that economic globalization is destined during the foreseeable future to undermine the capacity of states to exercise authority within their own domains.

At the same time, other forms of connectivity are generating growing threats to the capacity of states to exercise control over their internal affairs. Prominent in this regard are the impacts of climate change, the spread of infectious diseases across international boundaries, and the growing influence of social media. What analysts of complex systems treat as telecoupling is a particularly prominent feature of climate change (Liu et al. 2015). Temperature increases in the high latitudes play a role in the occurrence of severe droughts and extreme weather events in the mid-latitudes; global sea level rise is causing powerful storm surges that batter low-lying coastal areas and threaten the continued existence of some small-island states. With a few notable exceptions, states have demonstrated little capacity to control the spread of COVID-19 across their borders. There is nothing new about the spread of plagues from one region to another (McNeill 1976). But globalization has clearly made it more difficult to control infectious diseases that can spread globally in a matter of hours or days rather than weeks or months. There are good reasons to conclude that COVID-19 is only the tip of the iceberg in this realm. Social media provide large numbers of people with instant access to an extraordinary array of information (including disinformation) on a global basis. China's efforts to control the access of its citizens to social media through the creation and strengthening of the Great Firewall indicate that determined political leaders are by no means helpless in the face of the growth of social media (Klimburg 2017). Nevertheless, the overall effect of the ongoing cascade of innovations in the realm of social media is to raise the stakes dramatically for the leaders of states endeavoring to sustain their ability to exercise effective control over their internal affairs.

It is fair to conclude that the jury is out at this stage regarding the impacts of heightened connectivity as a systemic force in the global political order. What is clear is that states face higher hurdles not only in pursuing their goals in interactions with one another but also in maintaining their ability to govern effectively within the limits of their own jurisdictions. All but the largest and most powerful states find themselves increasingly at the mercy of impacts of telecoupling they are unable to control. It is possible as a result that the prevailing order will evolve over time into a system of states that are sovereign in name only. Experience regarding the late stages of other political orders as assessed by analysts like Oswald Spengler and Arnold Toynbee suggests that situations of this sort can continue for relatively long periods of time, without triggering the onset of a critical transition (Toynbee 1946; Spengler 2021). Nevertheless, such conditions increase vulnerability to the occurrence of tipping events that are difficult to anticipate but that can trigger cascades of changes eventuating in critical transitions or bifurcations in short order.

4.2 Virtual Reality

What may turn out to be the most profound development of the current era is the digital revolution giving rise to a world in which more and more human activities take place in cyberspace in contrast to material or physical space (Brousseau et al. 2012; DeNardis 2014; Slaughter 2017; Young et al. 2020). Increased connectivity is one among a wide range of consequences of this revolution. But the critical feature of this development with regard to the prevailing global order is that more and more human activities take place largely or wholly within the domain of virtual reality in contrast to physical reality. Humans are able to engage in a rapidly growing array of activities with little or no reference to their location in spatial terms and in a manner that sidesteps or simply ignores the rules and regulations enacted by spatially delimited actors such as states. With the ever-increasing sophistication of artificial intelligence, moreover, nonhuman agents are able to take on a variety of functions (e.g. intelligence gathering and synthesis, military operations) traditionally requiring intensive effort on the part of human actors (Lee 2021; Lee and Chen 2021; Metz 2021). There are many unknowns concerning what lies in store regarding the role of virtual reality as an organizing principle for human affairs. But without getting into speculative matters like the prospects for what is known as the technological singularity, it is apparent that the rise of virtual reality has restructured the landscape profoundly regarding political order on a global scale (Reese 2018; Young et al. 2020).

The idea of the global order as a state-based system rests on an understanding of states as place-based social units. They have jurisdictional boundaries that can be delimited in spatial terms and defended effectively against intrusions on the part of outsiders. States are expected to be able to exercise control over activities occurring within their domestic jurisdictions. Those residing within the boundaries of a state are assumed to think of themselves first and foremost as citizens (or resident aliens) of that state who accept the authority of the state to make legally binding decisions and recognize that they are obligated to comply with these decisions under normal circumstances. Of course, states vary in the extent to which they are able to fulfill these expectations for a variety of reasons. We are familiar with failed states that have lost the ability to govern effectively within their own jurisdictions, and we know that citizens do not always comply with rules promulgated by authorities even in well-ordered societies. But the rise of virtual reality seems transformative precisely because it raises questions about the extent to which place-based social units will continue to be able to act as the basic building blocks of the global political order in the future. We may be moving toward a world in which humans identify with social units located in cyberspace as much or more than they do with states. Perhaps more realistically, there are good reasons to expect that we are entering into a world populated by a mix of place-based and virtual social units that sometimes interact in a cooperative manner but also have interests that pull in competing directions under a variety of circumstances (DeNardis 2020).

This is not to suggest that states lack the ability to launch counterattacks against the growing influence of virtual reality. States can and often do make use of digital technologies themselves in their efforts to exercise effective control within their domestic jurisdictions (Klimburg 2017). In this regard, the case of China bears watching closely. China has invested heavily in the erection of what has become known as the Great Firewall as a means to regulate the extent to which Chinese citizens are able to interact freely in cyberspace with those located in other parts of the world. China also makes use of advanced technologies, such as facial recognition algorithms and digital accounting systems, in an effort to maintain the control of the state over the actions of its citizens. There is no doubt that these measures are effective under some conditions. Many observers outside China are skeptical regarding the ultimate effects of these measures. But this may be more an expression of distaste regarding Chinese practices than an informed judgment regarding the efficacy of these practices. At the same time, it is doubtful whether governments in most other states would be able to pursue a similar strategy effectively, even if some of their leaders are motivated to do so. Perhaps the most reasonable conclusion at this stage is that we are likely to see increased competition between place-based actors and virtual agents in the coming years and that it is difficult at this stage to forecast how this competition will play out.

A somewhat related development concerns the extent to which digital technologies allow outsiders to intervene in the internal affairs of states. Under the general rubric of cyber security, this has become a focus of intense interest in many quarters in recent years (Perlroth 2020). Of course, states can and do make use of digital technologies to protect and promote their own interests (Kello 2017). We are moving into an age in which it is possible to fight wars with few if any humans setting foot on the battlefield. States can also use digital technologies to interfere with the operation of the political systems of their adversaries and to pursue their economic goals remotely.

More striking in some respects, however, is the extent to which nonstate actors, including sophisticated individuals endowed with modest resources, are able to make use of digital technologies not only to escape the control of states but also to degrade the capacity of states to maintain control over their own affairs (Perlroth 2020). Using ransomware, malware, and other digital devices, hackers are now able not only to engage in identity theft, bullying, and various types of fraud but also to disrupt the activities of large corporations, hospitals and related health-care facilities, and government agencies. And there is no convincing reason to believe that governments are likely to gain the upper hand in the resultant offense–defense race. Increasingly, we find ourselves operating in a world in which both personal and public security is threatened, and the ability of governments to provide a reasonable measure of security within their own domains is compromised.

It is fair to conclude that we are still in the midst of the digital revolution. The rise of virtual reality has already shifted the ground dramatically regarding many aspects of the prevailing political order. But there are good reasons to expect that many more innovations, particularly in the realm of artificial intelligence, will come on stream during the coming years (Dauvergne 2020; Lee and Chen 2021). Whether the global order as we have known it in recent times can survive the impact of these developments intact remains to be seen. But at a minimum, we can expect a flow of developments that pose severe challenges to the resilience of the prevailing global political order. Periods of this kind deserve careful scrutiny because they feature many circumstances in which nonlinear events can trigger cascades of change leading to critical transitions or bifurcations. Such events are likely to take us by surprise even under these conditions. But there is a lot to be said for being prepared to be surprised.

4.3 A New Class of Problems

What I characterized at the outset as the twenty-first century's grand challenges of planetary governance are global issues that transcend conventional jurisdictional boundaries and that present unprecedented needs for governance that are difficult – perhaps impossible – to address effectively within the institutional framework provided by the prevailing global order. Challenges of this sort visible today include anthropogenic interference in the Earth's climate system, the spread of infectious diseases on a global scale, the escalating problems often grouped under the heading of cyber security, and the profound ethical issues associated with the revolution in biotechnology. The future is likely to feature additions to this class of unprecedented challenges.

The underlying issues embedded in these challenges giving rise to needs for governance are not all the same; they are rooted in several differentiable types of problems (Young 1997). Protecting the Earth's climate system is in essence a massive collective-action problem in which individual states are tempted by the hope that others will assume responsibility for reducing emissions of greenhouse gases, so that they and their citizens can enjoy the benefits of a stable climate system while acting as free riders with regard to contributing to the effort needed to achieve this result. In the absence of powerful incentives, there is a constant risk that states will fail to make good on paper commitments or pledges regarding the reduction of emissions of greenhouse gases needed to avoid serious disruption of the Earth's climate system, even when their promises take the form of explicit though nonlegally binding pledges of the sort exemplified by the Nationally Determined Contributions individual states have pledged to make under the terms of the 2015 Paris Climate Agreement.

In the case of pandemics, the anarchical character of the prevailing state-based society provides incentives for members to turn inward in a narrowly self-interested and short-sighted effort to erect barriers intended to shield themselves from the spread of infectious diseases arising in neighboring states, while blaming others for any failures to contain the spread of diseases across their borders (Kahl and Wright 2021). The problem is that such efforts are doomed to fail in a system featuring hyper-connectivity of the sort present on a global scale today. The multiplicity of disease vectors associated with the movement of people and goods across jurisdictional boundaries ensures that "we are all in this together" when it comes to controlling the spread of infectious diseases (Morrison 2022). Even China, with its unusual capacity to exercise control over its population, is experiencing increasing difficulties in implementing its zero COVID-19 policy effectively.

States themselves are implicated in some disruptive uses of digital technologies. Though leaders regularly issue denials and the evidence is hard to nail down conclusively, there are good reasons to conclude that individual states are behind some of most destructive digital interventions of recent years (Higgins 2021). It is difficult to imagine a way to engage in effective arms control in this realm among states seeking to exploit all means to maximize their relative gains. But an equally challenging feature of this problem arises from the difficulties states experience in controlling the actions of rogue individuals or small groups of unauthorized agents who are finding new ways to make use of these technologies to pursue antisocial ends, ranging from cyber bullying and identity theft to bringing down the computer systems that control the activities of major utilities like hospitals, pipelines, and power grids (Dauvergne 2020).

For its part, guiding developments in what is becoming known as the age of synthetic biology is a matter of the extent to which states have the capacity to steer the development and application of knowledge in areas where rapid advances have the potential, at one and the same time, to be used for socially beneficial purposes and for purposes that are harmful or at least outside the realm of socially acceptable applications (Webb and Hessel 2022). A particularly challenging feature of this challenge that is already on the horizon arises from the fact that germline editing is opening up the prospect of introducing heritable changes in the genetic makeup of human beings (Davies 2020; Evans 2020; Isaacson 2021). And there are good reasons to anticipate that currently unforeseen advances in biotechnology will emerge in the coming decades. One thing the cases of digital technology and biotechnology share is the challenge of governing breakthroughs in scientific knowledge and associated technological applications that have great potential to improve human well-being but at the same time produce a variety of opportunities for antisocial applications on the part of those motivated to pursue their own ends without regard to the implications for the common good. Often described as the dual-use problem, this challenge calls for innovative approaches to governance beyond anything under consideration today.

What is common to all these challenges, however, is that it is hard to make progress in addressing them within the prevailing global order. The effort to come to terms with climate change using the tools available within this order to address systemic needs for governance presents a clearcut illustration of the sources of this difficulty. Starting with the signing of the UN Framework Convention on Climate Change (UNFCCC) in 1992, we have sought over the last three decades to address this challenge through the negotiation of international legally binding instruments that states agree to voluntarily and that they may or may not make a good faith effort to implement within their domestic political systems. Yet overall concentrations of greenhouse gases in the Earth's atmosphere have continued to rise rapidly, and we are now beginning to experience disruptive events that can be attributed unambiguously to climate change.[5] The concentration of carbon dioxide in the Earth's atmosphere now stands at ~415 ppm, and we are on a trajectory leading toward exceeding the temperature target articulated in general terms in the Framework Convention, spelled out more precisely in the 2015 Paris Climate Agreement, and sharpened to a limit of average temperature increases at the Earth's surface of no more than 1.5°C in the 2021 Glasgow Climate Pact. In the high latitudes of the northern

---

[5] The most authoritative source of data on greenhouse gas emissions and concentrations in the Earth's atmosphere is the Global Carbon Project's annual "Carbon Budget" report – www.globalcarbonproject.org.

hemisphere, temperature increases have already breached this barrier by a substantial margin, and policymakers concerned with Arctic issues are grappling with the challenges of adapting to a range of impacts of climate change.

Though counterfactuals are notoriously difficult to construct in this realm, it is possible to make a case that the situation we face today might well have been worse in the absence of the climate regime. In the wake of COP 26 in Glasgow in the fall of 2021, some have come to believe that policymakers in leading countries have finally recognized the seriousness of the problem of climate change and that they are beginning to respond appropriately. But it is not possible to argue that we have been able to meet the challenge of mitigation, much less the ensuing challenge of adaptation, effectively within the confines of the prevailing global order. In essence, this is attributable to the fact that meeting these challenges will require transformative changes in major features of the socioeconomic systems of advanced industrial societies, a level of adjustment that is seldom if ever possible to achieve through efforts to hammer out the specific provisions of international conventions or treaties.

We have less experience to evaluate when it comes to efforts to address the other grand challenges. There is a lack of international legally binding instruments in place to control the spread of infectious diseases, prevent antisocial uses of digital technologies, or guide uses of biotechnologies. An initiative designed to develop the terms of a "pandemic treaty" has begun (Phelan and Carlson 2022). But it is not likely that this effort will be any more successful than the effort to deal with climate change through the negotiation of legally binding instruments. Rather than taking steps to build a stronger international regime to address the spread of infectious diseases and enhancing the capacity of the World Health Organization to administer this regime, many states are busy blaming each other for the spread of COVID-19 and undermining the authority of the WHO (Cueto et al. 2019). Nor is the situation any more promising in the cases of coping with misuses of cyberspace and guiding the development of biotechnology. With regard to disruptive uses of digital technologies, in particular, states are part of the problem rather than part of the solution. While the revolution in biotechnology is shaping up as one of the most important scientific developments of the twenty-first century, states have barely begun to recognize the significance of this development from the perspective of governance.

An examination of the fate of large political orders of the past suggests that they commonly break down when they encounter challenges they are unable to address effectively. These challenges may arise from biophysical occurrences such as severe and prolonged droughts or from external sources like the impacts of European diseases coupled with the arrival of Spanish conquistadores that doomed the Aztec and Inca Empires in the sixteenth century. But they may also arise from internal socioeconomic developments that a prevailing political order is unable to cope with effectively. The state-based system itself originated in Europe in the seventeenth century in a setting in which the preexisting political order was unable to cope with forces unleashed by the Reformation and Counter-Reformation on the European Continent during the sixteenth century along with the outward expansion resulting from commercial and imperial ventures on the part of Spain and Portugal in the sixteenth century followed by the rise of Holland as a commercial power in the seventeenth century.

Are we reaching a similar juncture today on a global scale? While most of us take the existence of the prevailing state-based political order for granted on a day-to-day basis, history suggests that any such assumption is unwarranted. Political orders in individual societies rise and fall (Lebow 2018). In some cases, they hang on for considerable periods even after growing internal contradictions make it harder and harder for them to cope with rising challenges. Similar processes are at work in larger settings. The Peace of Westphalia ushering in the state-based system in Europe, for example, followed decades of highly destructive warfare that erupted from conflicts that had grown increasingly intractable through much of the sixteenth century (Wedgwood 2005). Whether we are motivated to find ways to enhance the resilience of the current global order or to take steps to accelerate the emergence of some alternative order that may take its place, there are good reasons at this stage to engage in systematic thinking about the fate of the prevailing order as we seek to find effective responses to the grand challenges of the twenty-first century.

5 Political Tipping Elements

The constitutive pressures and systemic forces I have examined in the preceding sections are impacting the prevailing global order substantially. Still, it seems correct to conclude at this juncture that the prevailing order remains a state-based system, and experience with complex systems suggests that this situation may last for some time. At the same time, complex systems experiencing conditions of this sort are prone to the occurrence of catalytic events triggering cascades of nonlinear changes leading to critical transitions or bifurcations. This suggests the value of applying our understanding of the roles of tipping elements, thresholds, and trigger mechanisms in complex systems to the case of the prevailing global order in an effort to shed light on the prospects for fundamental change in this order during the foreseeable future.

5.1 Resilience

The growing literature on resilience in socioecological systems has drawn our attention to the observation that many complex systems have some capacity to adapt to changing conditions and new challenges, adjusting their inner workings to continue operating effectively without experiencing critical transitions featuring transformative changes in their constitutive features (Gunderson and Holling 2002; Walker and Salt 2006). Resilience in this sense is a variable. Different systems may vary with regard to their level or degree of resilience. The same system may be more resilient in the face of some disruptive forces than others; it also may evolve in ways that either increase or decrease its resilience over the course of time. In the case of human systems including political orders, moreover, resilience is subject to the impact of human actions, whether planned or unplanned. Those who benefit from an existing order, are satisfied with the results it produces with regard to their own interests, or fear the consequence of critical transitions may engage in conscious efforts to enhance the resilience of the order or at least to blunt the impact of threats to its continuation. Those dissatisfied with the prevailing order, on the other hand, can be expected to act in ways that undermine the resilience of the order or, in any case, to make little or no effort to combat developments likely to erode its resilience. In both cases, such efforts may not prove effective. But this does not mean we can afford to ignore them in thinking about the dynamics of political orders. Human actions motivated by wholly different concerns, moreover, may produce impacts affecting the resilience of prevailing political orders that most actors fail to recognize or dismiss as unimportant.

How resilient is the global political order under the conditions prevailing today? The burgeoning literature on the resilience of socioecological systems is suffused with a general sense of optimism about the adaptive capacity of various types of systems as they confront both internal and external threats. Yet this is not an easy question to answer in the case of the current global order. As the debate about the decline of the state that took place in the 1970s and 1980s made clear, it would be a mistake to underestimate the staying power of states and the state-based system (Hoffmann 1966; Herz 1976). In the final analysis, strong states have both the authority and the capacity to exercise effective control over the activities of nonstate actors ranging from wealthy individuals to large multinational corporations. As I have observed, a striking example today involves the steps China is taking to impose effective restrictions on the actions of major corporate players. Nevertheless, the constitutive pressures and systemic forces I considered in the preceding sections are eroding some of the foundational elements of the current order. And it is increasingly apparent that the normal tools for responding to needs for governance within this order are severely limited when it comes to addressing the twenty-first century's grand challenges. Old orders have a tendency to linger on for more or less lengthy periods, even when they suffer a loss of effectiveness in addressing needs for governance. But a common pathway leading to the decline and ultimate collapse of political orders features an inability to come to terms with critical needs for governance. There is no reason to regard the current global order as exceptional in these terms.

5.2 Tipping Elements

An important analytical development in these terms involves what those seeking to understand the dynamics of complex systems have come to think of as tipping elements (Lenton et al. 2008; Scheffer et al. 2012; Lenton 2020). Tipping elements are mechanisms embedded in complex systems that once triggered can generate amplifying shock waves eventuating in the occurrence of critical transitions or bifurcations at the systemic level. A consideration of such tipping elements and the triggers that can activate them has emerged as a prominent feature of recent analyses of the Earth's climate system and, more generally, in the literature on what observers have come to regard as planetary boundaries (Pearce 2007; Rockström et al. 2009; McKay et al. 2022). In the case of the climate system, analysts point to mechanisms like the disintegration of the Greenland icecap, the collapse of the West Antarctic Ice Sheet, large releases of carbon dioxide and methane from thawing permafrost, or the destruction of the Amazonian rainforest as events that could trigger cascades of changes producing a state change departing from the Earth's climate system as we know it today and eventuating in the emergence of some fundamentally different system (Lenton et al. 2008). A particular concern in this connection is that the stable and relatively benign climate system of the last 10,000 years, the era known as the Holocene, may be replaced by a climate system that is more chaotic and that is difficult for humans to adapt to easily (Mayewski et al. 2004; Steffen et al. 2004). State changes in complex systems are difficult to anticipate; they generally take us by surprise. Nevertheless, they do occur from time to time producing consequences that ripple through the entire system. It is dangerous to ignore the significance of tipping elements just because we lack the ability to understand their behavior clearly.

The idea of tipping elements is helpful in understanding nonlinear changes in situations ranging from deterioration in the health of individual persons to the collapse of large socioecological systems. There is some literature on the application of ideas relating to complex systems to the global political order (Harrison 2007; Kavalski 2015; Orsini et al. 2020), and a number of observers have emphasized the significance of turbulence in the prevailing global order (Rosenau 1990). No one has made a sustained effort to make use of the idea of tipping elements to enhance our understanding of the dynamics of political orders. But it is not difficult to see the relevance of this line of thinking to efforts to understand developments leading to critical transitions in specific orders. Most accounts of the collapse of Indigenous political orders in North America following initial contacts with Europeans in the fifteenth and sixteenth centuries, for example, point to the ravages caused by the introduction of diseases like smallpox and measles that were not present in the region prior to contact with Europeans. Largescale urban uprisings in France, exemplified by the storming of the Bastille in July 1989 and its aftermath, seem to have provided the spark igniting powerful forces bringing down the *ancien regime*, which had been ailing for some time but managed to keep going as a consequence of inertia in the absence of a spark igniting a cascade of developments leading to a critical transition. As these examples suggest, it is helpful in thinking about nonlinear changes in complex systems to consider the role of triggers in the sense of seemingly discrete events that activate tipping elements and set in motion processes leading to critical transitions or bifurcations.

5.3 Political Triggers

Can we identify tipping elements and potential triggers in the global political order today? This is largely uncharted territory from an analytic perspective; all suggestions about such matters should be regarded as preliminary observations. Even so, we can identify mechanisms that are likely candidates for the status of tipping elements and triggers in the prevailing order, so long as we bear in mind that the examples I describe in the next several paragraphs remain tentative at this stage and that they certainly do not constitute an exhaustive list of potential tipping elements and triggers in the prevailing order.

A war beginning as a localized armed clash that escalates into a conflict between two or more major powers and eventuates in the use of weapons of mass destruction leaving large urban centers in ruins could trigger a series of events putting an end to the state-based system as we know it. As those who have developed the idea of nuclear winter have observed, there is a distinct possibility that a major nuclear war could make the planet uninhabitable for many species including *Homo sapiens* for a more-or-less protracted period of time (Robock 2010). But even short of this, such a war could destroy the capacity of major players in the current system to govern effectively within their own jurisdictions and produce a widespread sense of the bankruptcy of the prevailing order. The emergence of climate change and the other grand challenges of the twenty-first century has resulted in a tendency to push the threat of nuclear war to the back burner in thinking about the future of the global order. But this is almost certainly a mistake. The great powers show no signs of a willingness to relinquish their arsenals of nuclear weapons. On the contrary, they are engaging in well-funded research and development efforts yielding a variety of new weapons systems featuring nuclear warheads. Nuclear prolif-eration has proceeded more slowly than many analysts anticipated several decades ago. But the knowledge needed to build nuclear weapons is in general circulation; numerous states have the capacity to produce such weapons in relatively short order, and there is no basis for confidence in the continued effectiveness of the nuclear nonproliferation regime or some realistic alterna-tive. The Ukraine crisis is a forceful reminder that the danger of armed clashes escalating to nuclear exchanges is real.

Similar remarks are in order regarding the impacts of a sharp shift from the benign and remarkably stable climate system of the Holocene to a considerably more variable and harsh climate system. Although we seldom give the matter much thought, the Earth's climate system over the last 10,000 years, roughly the period spanning the development of what we regard as human civilization, has been remarkably favorable to the development of large and increasingly advanced human settlements. There is no guarantee that these conditions will continue, especially if we are unable to achieve drastic reductions in anthropo-genic emissions of greenhouse gases over the next two or three decades. Most accounts of climate change focus on relatively gradual shifts in temperatures at the Earth's surface, sea levels, and so forth. But it is perfectly possible that transgressing planetary boundaries will trigger sharp shifts in key features of the Earth's climate system and a variety of increasingly extreme events. The disintegration of the Greenland icecap, for example, would raise sea levels on a global basis some six to seven meters. The global order in its current form has little capacity to cope with sharp shifts of this sort. The result could well be drastic disruptions in existing societies, large migrations of climate refugees across existing political boundaries, and a general decline in the Earth's carry-ing capacity for human beings.

Another tipping element in the current global order centers on the rapid spread of one or more infectious diseases of a sort that would make COVID-19 seem mild by comparison. Many observers place our experience with COVID-19 on a par with the major disruptive events of the twentieth century, including the world wars and the Great Depression. These were certainly dramatic shocks to the system. Yet none of them precipitated a critical transition in the state-based system. The final decades of the twentieth century witnessed the globalization of the state-based system, and there is no indication that

COVID-19 is producing a sharp decline in the authority of states. Yet those with expertise regarding the emergence and spread of infectious diseases have made it clear that the eruption of an infectious disease considerably more destructive than COVID-19 is a distinct possibility (Snowden 2019). Judging from recent experience, those in positions of authority are profoundly unprepared for the occurrence of such an event. It is impossible to say with any confidence how lethal an infectious disease would have to be to trigger a cascade of events leading to a critical transition in the prevailing order. But the plausibility of a tipping element of this sort is hard to deny.

Yet another example features what we may think of as a descent into chaos in cyberspace. The growth of the Internet and the worldwide web over the last fifty years as systems that have become prominent features of our lives in the absence of a formalized governance system has produced a sense that the rise of virtual reality does not present a serious challenge to the prevailing global order (Isaacson 2014). But there is no basis for taking the generally benign consequences of digital technologies for granted (DeNardis 2014). It is not difficult to imagine an uncontrollable dynamic in which the norms and practices associated with the rise of digital technologies break down under the weight of a cascade of escalating misuses of digital technologies. States themselves may contribute to this dangerous development as they engage in a digital arms race involving applications of advanced technologies to promote their national interests. And the growing capacity of a wide range of nonstate actors to use digital technologies for antisocial purposes is hard to ignore. None of this is to say that such a sequence of events is inevitable. But it seems reasonable to treat this prospect as a tipping element in the prevailing political order.

6 The Effects of Scale

Suppose a critical transition in the global political order does occur during the coming years or decades. What can we say about the defining features of a potential successor to the current order? In the remaining sections of this Element, I address this question with particular reference to the implications of such a transition for efforts to address the class of unprecedented needs for governance that I have characterized as the grand challenges of planetary governance.

6.1 The Nature of Scale

A subject that deserves special consideration in this connection centers on the effects of scale. Put simply, the conventional wisdom regarding scale is that as political orders grow in size, they require more centralized and more authoritative institutional arrangements to address needs for governance construed as a social function centered on steering societies away from collectively undesirable outcomes and toward desirable ones. On this account, governance without government may be a viable option in small settings featuring limited numbers of relatively homogeneous actors. But as we move toward larger and more complex systems, the need for what we ordinarily think of as a government able to exercise authority effectively rises. How persuasive is this argument in thinking about what it will take to address the twenty-first century's grand challenges of planetary governance?

It is helpful to start by drawing distinctions among several scalar dimensions relevant to thinking about the dynamics of political orders (Gibson et al. 2000). In terms of spatial scale, political orders range from the micro-level involving a few tens of square kilometers through a variety of intermediate levels to the macro-level encompassing the planet as a whole and the atmospheric envelope affected by human actions. In the case of demographic scale, political orders cover a spectrum ranging from a few dozens or hundreds of people to the almost eight billion humans alive today. With regard to economic scale, it makes sense to think of political orders ranging from the simplest subsistence systems through more complex agrarian systems and on up to the advanced industrialized system in operation today at the global level.

The prevailing global order is an extreme case with regard to all these scalar dimensions. It covers the entire planet together with those segments of space affected by human actions, including the deployment of satellites and the impacts of airborne pollutants. This order encompasses all human beings as well as all other living species impacted by human actions. It features a global economic system in which advanced technologies, including both conventional and digital technologies, are prominent elements of the system. These features of the global political order will remain the same, whether or not the state-based system gives way to some alternative form of political order. It is to be expected that human activities will expand during the foreseeable future to encompass a larger swath of space. But in essence, the global political order of the future will involve what we often speak of today as Earth system governance (Biermann 2014; Earth System Governance Project 2018).

6.2 The Challenge of Scale

The pivotal issue in the discussion of the effects of scale has to do with the relationship between scale and the need for a government endowed with the authority to make collective choices that are binding on those subject to its jurisdiction and possessing the capacity to ensure a reasonably high level of compliance with these decisions. Can small political orders avoid the need for centralized authority? Are there ways to structure large orders that avoid or at least significantly reduce the need for an overarching government? Does the introduction of increasingly sophisticated digital technologies and the growing importance of virtual reality open up opportunities to devise effective arrangements capable of addressing the function of governance in the absence of government even in large orders?

Studies of small political orders reveal that humans have come up with a wide range of solutions to the challenge of addressing needs for governance. Powerful leaders emerge to make collective choices and impose them on others in some settings. But there are also cases in which arrangements featuring governance without government prove effective in handling needs for governance (Ostrom 1990). More complex arrangements are also common (Graeber and Wengrow 2021). In some settings, responsibility for making collective choices is distributed, so that some people are recognized as authoritative with regard to particular functions, while others are accorded authority in other realms. This typically reflects the fact that different members of the community have expertise or exceptional skills regarding specific activities of common concern. Some small social groups come together in larger numbers during certain seasons of the year but disperse into subgroups during other seasons. In such cases, governance systems are adapted to these seasonal rhythms. Some systems feature well-defined gender roles, according women authority to make collective decisions in some areas, while men have the authority to make such decisions in other areas. Overall, the principal conclusion to be drawn from the record is that there is great diversity among small societies with regard to the arrangements they develop to address needs for governance (Ostrom 2005).

The usual assumption is that once societies become larger in spatial and demographic terms and more advanced in economic terms, the need for an assemblage of institutions recognizable as a government in the normal sense grows. A conventional interpretation suggests that the agricultural revolution and the growth of sizable year round human settlements led more or less directly to the establishment of governments (Scott 2017).[6] Though there is

---

[6] A note on terminology is in order here. I use the term state to refer to social units that meet the requirements for membership in the state-based system. Many anthropological and historical accounts, on the other hand, speak of the state in reference to a centralized body that has the authority and the capacity to make collective decisions on behalf of social units. On this account, an anarchical society, such as the current global order, is a stateless society. To avoid confusion, I use the term government to refer to such a centralized body. To speak of the state-based system as anarchical, therefore, is to observe that there is no global or world government in this system.

considerable controversy about such matters, most analysts treat this as a matter, at least in part, of the growing complexity of these larger systems and the resultant need for more sophisticated procedures for handling the function of governance. But it is also worth noting that the production of a surplus over and above subsistence needs provides the resources required to support the activities of a class of administrators. On this account, social evolution has continued to increase the prominence of governments, whether those who administer them are authoritarian leaders who seize power or are chosen by the members of society through some sort of democratic or participatory process. There is great diversity among the universe of governments (Ostrom 2005). Some prove effective and resilient; others fail and are replaced by new governments either through peaceful means or as a consequence of violent actions. But the mainstream narrative in this realm is that there is a clearcut relationship between scale and the role of government. The higher the level in terms of spatial, demographic, and economic scale, the greater the need for an effective government.

Recent scholarship, however, has raised fundamental questions about the validity of this mainstream narrative regarding human social evolution, suggesting that it may be better understood as a reflection of conventional western thinking than as an assessment of the human experience more generally. For one thing, there is growing evidence in the historical record that relatively large human societies have arisen in different times and places and have persisted over long periods of time in the absence of anything we can identify as a government in the ordinary sense of the term (Graeber and Wengrow 2021). Some of this evidence points to the political orders created by various groups of Indigenous peoples and persisting over long periods of time. The Five Nations of the Haudenosaunee (also known as the Iroquois Confederation), for example, brought together several distinct groups in a loose confederation that lacked anything recognizable as a central government but that nevertheless proved effective in meeting essential needs for governance over a long period of time. But the relevant cases are not limited to political orders arising among Indigenous peoples. The idea of the Middle Kingdom in China, for example, directs attention to a political order arising around 1000 CE that did not feature a comprehensive central government in the ordinary western sense of the term.

Even among western analysts, there is a significant stream of thinking that raises serious questions about the conventional wisdom regarding the effects of scale. The eighteenth-nineteenth-century anarchist philosophers William Godwin, Pierre-Joseph Proudhon, and Peter Kropotkin, for instance, adopted a relatively benign view of human nature and argued that large human societies are capable of developing informal practices that allow people to live together in harmony or at least peacefully in the absence of the coercive pressures associated with the efforts of governments to enforce rules on subjects who have little or no incentive to comply with them on a voluntary basis (Proudhon 2011; Godwin 2013; Kropotkin 2014). The libertarians of the twentieth century developed arguments only slightly more favorable to the need for a government in the ordinary sense. Analysts like Friedrich Hayek, for example, developed a minimalist perspective in which the role of government could and should be limited to the role of night watchman or, at most, referee ensuring that players act in accordance with the rules of the game (Hayek 1973). So long as the actors play by the rules, on this account, we should make no effort to interfere with the right of individual actors to do as they please or to alter the outcomes of their interactions in accordance with some ideas of distributive justice or fairness (Nozick 1974). This line of thinking resonates with a significant group of current thinkers, though they are by no means blind to the problems associated with such views (Scott 2012).

The attraction of such perspectives is amplified by the observation that governments are often dysfunctional or, worse yet, succumb to the control of authoritarian leaders pursuing some odious ideology or seeking to aggrandize themselves at the expense of the general public. There is no doubt that these concerns are real. Even in systems generally regarded as democratic, the weight of bureaucracy can lead to extreme inefficiency or, in the worst case, bring the activities of government agencies to a standstill. One result is a loss of resilience in the sense of the capacity to adapt effectively to changing biophysical or socioeconomic conditions. The difficulties many societies experience in devising effective responses to the impacts of climate change provide a prominent case in point. In other cases, governments lose the ability to exercise authority altogether, leading to the emergence of what we have come to think of as failed states. And as the experiences of the twentieth century made clear in a particularly vivid way, totalitarian systems can brutalize their own citizens and engage in reckless actions that precipitate large wars with other states and massive famines at home. Under the circumstances, it is not difficult to understand why analysts like Hayek writing in the 1940s referred to the growth of big government as putting us on "the road to serfdom" (Hayek 1944).

6.3 Governance without Government

The case of the state-based system appears to run directly counter to the general view that the need for a central government rises as the scale of a political order grows. Given the constitutive features of this system, the emergence of a central government possessing the authority and the capacity to make and implement collective choices binding on the member states would involve a critical transition from the prevailing order to some new form of political order. Some analysts have produced arguments suggesting that the normal relationship between scale and the need for a government do not apply in the case of the global political order. This is where ideas regarding the role of the balance of power, the English School's concept of solidarism, what Ostrom and others call polycentric arrangements, and the vision of governance without government come into play (Bull 1977; Rosenau and Czempiel 1992; Dietz et al. 2003; Linklater and Suganami 2006; Ostrom 2010; Aligica and Tarko 2012; Thiel et al. 2019). Nevertheless, there is no getting around the conclusion that the creation of a central government would be incompatible with our understanding of the constitutive features of the prevailing order.

There have been efforts to chip away at the margins in this regard. The most significant example involves the idea of collective security articulated in the provisions of Chapter VII of the Charter of the United Nations adopted in 1945 at the close of World War II (Claude 1962). The essence of this idea is that member states should accept some limitations on their sovereignty with regard to situations involving "threats to the peace, breaches of the peace, and acts of aggression." The Charter grants authority to the UN Security Council to make decisions that are binding on the member states regarding matters of this sort. Nevertheless, it would be a mistake to exaggerate the significance of this development. For starters, the Charter accords each of the five permanent members of the Security Council – the victors in World War II – the right to veto any resolution it is unwilling to support. In effect, this means that what looks like a system involving a distinctive system of collective security is in reality more like an institutionalized form of great-power politics in which balance of power considerations play a central role (Claude 1962; Bull 1977).

What is more, even the relatively modest provisions of Chapter VII have not been implemented as envisioned by the drafters of the Charter. The gap between the ideal and the actual in this regard is large; divisions among the permanent members have stymied UN intervention in many dangerous or disruptive situations, including the recent military hostilities in Ukraine. This is not to say that the United Nations has played no role with regard to matters of peace and security. Innovative practices in the realm of what has become known as peacekeeping are particularly notable. But it seems safe to say that whatever the intentions of those who drafted the Charter, the operation of the United Nations in practice has not produced anything resembling a critical transition in the character of the prevailing global order.

For a long time, some analysts have argued that we are in need of a world government to address international needs for governance effectively (Clark and Sohn 1962). Those who make such arguments are saying in effect that we need to abandon the state-based system in favor of an alternative form of political order. Most analysts of world affairs have dismissed such arguments as visionary; they conclude that these arguments fall well outside the boundaries of what they regard as realistic proposals for addressing needs for governance on a global scale. They may be right in adopting this view, so long as we assume that there is little or no prospect of the occurrence of a critical transition in the existing order. Nevertheless, this interpretation fails to confront the issues associated with the twenty-first century's grand challenges of planetary governance. As a result, we are left with the following questions. Are the grand challenges likely to undermine the standard arguments of those who defend the state-based system as a political order capable of addressing needs for governance at the global level? If so, is it possible to imagine an alternative order capable of coming to terms with the grand challenges, without generating what many observers have identified as likely negative side effects associated with the creation of a world government?

7 The Global Political Order of the Future

Should the prevailing political order experience a critical transition or what those who think about complex systems regard as a bifurcation in contrast to an oscillation, what can we say about the character of its successor? There is no straightforward answer to this question. Nonlinear changes constitute the norm in complex systems; surprise is a central feature of developments occurring in such settings. This makes both the timing and the trajectory of such changes difficult to anticipate, much less to forecast with any confidence. There is no shortage of pundits ready and willing to proclaim their views regarding the character of the global political order of the future. Without exception, however, their prognostications turn out to be of little help in guiding our thinking about a successor to the state-based system.

Still, this does not mean we must throw up our hands and forego all efforts to think rigorously about the global political order of the future. Taking the discussion of constitutive pressure points and systemic forces in earlier sections of this Element as a point of departure, I consider in this section a series of central questions pertaining to this issue. The result is not a prediction or a collection of predictions regarding what lies in store in this realm. But the discussion may help to structure our thinking about the global political order of the future in a productive fashion.

7.1 The Pace of Change

There is a pronounced tendency to think of critical transitions or bifurcations as sudden occurrences. On this account, crossing a systemic threshold or passing a tipping point is like flipping a switch; the shift from one state to another seems to be a cataclysmic event catapulting us into a dramatically different situation almost overnight. Some critical transitions do fit this conception of change. In any case, they are commonly presented in such a way that they seem to have the character of cataclysms, whether or not this is an accurate depiction of what actually transpired. Many accounts of the collapse of the *ancien regime* in France in 1789; the outbreak of World War I in 1914; the stock market crash in 1929 precipitating the Great Depression, and the disintegration of the Soviet Union in 1991, for example, fit this mold. But it is easy to exaggerate this perspective on critical transitions. In many cases, we are surprised mainly because we have not been paying close attention to the dynamics of the relevant system. Those who were paying attention knew that the *ancien regime* in France had become a house of cards by the final decades of the eighteenth century and that the deterioration of the Soviet order had progressed to the point where it would have taken more than *perestroika* to put this system on an even keel by the time Mikhail Gorbachev came to power in 1985.

One insight arising from these observations is that there may be opportunities to exercise some influence over the trajectory of a critical transition, even in cases where there is no way to forestall the unfolding of such a transition over the course of time. Even in cases where it is possible to see that transformation has become a likely occurrence, it is hard to forecast the ignition of the spark that precipitates the actual shift. At the beginning of 1789, no one was in a position to anticipate the urban uprising in Paris featuring the storming of the Bastille in July of that year; similar remarks are in order regarding the failed conservative putsch that occurred in Moscow in the summer of 1991 leading to the disintegration of the Soviet Union by the end of the year. Much the same is true regarding the fate of the global political order today. It is not hard to see that there are fundamental questions about the resilience of this order in its current form. But if and when a spark ignites a cascade of changes leading to the rise of a new global order, we are almost certain to be taken by surprise.

7.2 Alternative Paradigms

Even so, this does not mean there is nothing of interest to say about the forces likely to shape the character of a successor to the current global political order. For one thing, the global order as we know it today is rooted in western thinking highlighting the idea that there is a need to enter into an enforceable social contract to avoid the dismal condition envisioned in the idea of a Hobbesian state of nature and emphasizing the idea of what we regard as the rule of law as the way to create and administer a social contract well-suited to the circumstances at hand (Graeber and Wengrow 2021). It is true that the current order is anarchical in the sense that it lacks a central public authority able to make laws or legally binding agreements and to ensure that they are implemented to lend order to day-to-day interactions among the members of this system. Still, there are constant calls for strengthening what popular accounts refer to as the rules-based order; the negotiation of legally binding instruments is widely regarded as the appropriate way to address issues ranging from arms control and trade to human rights and climate change (Chayes and Chayes 1995). The negotiation of the provisions of what emerged at the end of WWII as the legally binding Charter of the United Nations represents a kind of high water mark for this way of thinking about global political order. The Charter sets forth a system of governance that comes as close as possible to fulfilling the western ideal of the rule of law on a global basis, without actually displacing the principles of internal and external sovereignty that remain constitutive features of the current order (Claude 1959).

There is no reason to assume that a successor to the prevailing order will be based on these western ideals regarding preferred forms of governance. For one thing, we are witnessing what many now regard as the decline of the West (Morris 2010; Dalio 2021). This is not so much a matter of the erosion of the dominant role of the United States as the leader of the West as it is a shift in world views to reflect the influence of other conceptions of political order and especially those embedded in non-western cultures like those of China and India (Wang 2017; Zhao 2019). The point is not that some particular non-western perspective on political order will become dominant on a global scale any time soon. But it is a fair bet that the global political order of the future will not conform to some updated western vision.

This observation is reinforced by the fact that it seems difficult and perhaps impossible to come to terms with what I call the grand challenges of the twenty-first century using familiar western strategies for meeting needs for governance. The shortcomings associated with the effort to address the problem of climate change through the negotiation of international legally binding instruments provide a dramatic example. It is now thirty years since the signing of the UNFCCC. During that time, the climate problem has become more severe. Globally, average temperatures at the Earth's surface have increased ~1.1°C over preindustrial levels; temperatures in the Arctic are rising at roughly three to four times this rate. We are on track toward global increases of 2.5–3°C during the course of this century, despite efforts to strengthen the climate regime on the part of representatives of states meeting annually at the Conference of the Parties of the UNFCCC and resulting most recently in the 2021 Glasgow Climate Pact. And this assumes we do not cross a threshold or boundary leading to rapid nonlinear changes in the Earth's climate system. It is understandable, under the circumstances, that we now speak of the climate emergency rather than the problem of climate change. The other grand challenges identified in the preceding sections are at least as difficult to address effectively using the familiar repertoire of governance strategies available within the prevailing order (Phelan and Carlson 2022).

Today's order is rooted in physical reality in the sense that its members are treated as territorial units whose boundaries are delimited in spatial or geographical terms and whose governments have jurisdiction over activities occurring within these boundaries. But the digital revolution has brought with it a dramatic growth in virtual reality as the medium in which more and more human activities take place. States can and do endeavor to make use of their authority and coercive capacity to regulate human activities taking place in cyberspace. The current tensions between various governments and Meta (formerly Facebook), which has 2.9 billion users worldwide who employ social media to pursue social and antisocial goals even when they conflict with regulatory measures enacted by states, constitutes a striking example of the difficulties states encounter in seeking to control activities in cyberspace. And this is simply the tip of the iceberg. The development of new digital technologies, especially in the realm of artificial intelligence, is accelerating rapidly (Dauvergne 2020; Crawford 2021; Lee 2021). As people spend more of their lives in cyberspace and engage in a wide range of transactions using virtual currencies, it will become harder and harder for place-based units to exercise control over the trajectories of societies effectively.

Still, we should avoid rushing to hasty judgments in this realm. China's energetic efforts to build a Great Firewall allowing the state to exercise control over the information available to its citizens and to make use of advanced technologies (e.g. facial recognition software) to track the activities of citizens in real time as a means of asserting social control constitutes a particularly interesting experiment in these terms. In an important sense, China may be emerging as a bastion of conservatism in terms of efforts to shore up the state-based system as a political order in which territorial states endeavor to exercise effective control over all activities occurring within their jurisdictional boundaries. It is far too early to pass judgment on the likely results of China's experiment in social control over the next several decades. But whatever happens in China, there is little likelihood that China's approach to the regulation of virtual reality will take root throughout much of the rest of the Earth system. At a minimum, this means that a range of actors that differ in fundamental ways from territorial states will play roles of growing importance in the global political order of the future.

7.3 Membership

The idea of a political order in which membership is limited to a single class of social units and all members are treated as equals has a certain appeal; it certainly simplifies things when it comes to the development of prescriptions applicable to the behavior of members. As noted, membership in the state-based system is limited to sovereign states, and all states are regarded as equal in juridical terms, regardless of their differences in numerous other respects. All other actors are lumped into the residual category of nonstate actors and assumed to be subordinate to states in the sense that they are subject to the laws of the states within whose jurisdiction they operate. For their part, all states are eligible for membership in the United Nations where they all have a single vote (with the exception of the veto accorded to the permanent members of the Security Council). The result is that the UN General Assembly can and often does pass resolutions without the concurrence of one or more of the great powers, though the constitutive principle of external sovereignty ensures that these resolutions are not considered binding on those states that do not vote for them.

The idea that all members of the prevailing order are equal is simply a convenient fiction in most respects. States range from superpowers, like the United States and China, capable of exercising effective influence over others regarding many issues, to micro-states, like Andorra, Kiribati, and Vanuatu, that have little influence and may even find their land base eroded by the impacts of climate change. While major states can and do send delegations comprising hundreds of members to international events such as the annual meeting of the Conference of the Parties of the UNFCCC, micro-states lack the resources to staff diplomatic missions in other countries, much less to send sizable delegations to major international meetings. Ironically, some of these states regularly turn to nonstate actors for assistance needed to participate meaningfully in international meetings. For example, major environmental organizations often provide staff support for the representatives of small-island states in settings like the UNFCCC Conference of the Parties. Even so, there is something appealing about a society of states in which all members are treated as equals, operating within the framework of a uniform system of international laws and diplomatic practices.

When it comes to thinking about the global political order of the future, on the other hand, there is no reason to assume that membership would need to be restricted to a single category of actors. Considering the general class of political orders, it is apparent that many orders are or have been populated with distinct classes of actors that are subject to differentiated rights and rules. Of course, democracies cling to the often threadbare premise that all their members are citizens and that all citizens are equal in political and legal terms. But beyond this, distinctions among types or classes of members seem to be the order of the day rather than the exception. Think of traditional systems in which there are warriors, priests, merchants, and peasants occupying distinct roles or arrangements like the long-established Indian caste system in which the rules of the game applying to members of individual castes differ profoundly.[7] Perhaps more to the point in this discussion is the European order that preceded the state-based system in which the members included commercial cities, principalities, proto-states, the Holy Roman Empire, and religious organizations like the Catholic Holy See (Jones 2021). Needless to say, sorting out the relationships between and among these actors was a complex and often messy business. But even in a setting in which communication was slow and often untrustworthy, the major players became adept in finding ways to cope with this challenge.

Under conditions emerging today, the crucial distinction may be between place-based actors like territorial states seeking to maximize control over their subjects and actors rooted in cyberspace, including some virtual actors that may be motivated to engage in ethically questionable or antisocial uses of digital technologies. In between, there are numerous actors such as financial organizations and environmental organizations that do have a material presence but that also conduct much of their work in cyberspace (DeNardis 2020). It is difficult at this stage to say how interactions between and among these different types of actors will be ordered in the global political order of the future. But one thing is clear. It would be a mistake simply to assume that the authority to make and implement decisions about such matters will be granted to a single type of actor, as in the case of states in the current order. Sorting out this matter will be challenging; it may be some time before the terms of a new global political order are translated into established practices. But that is not to say that it cannot be done.

7.4 Structure

The idea that the members of any future global political order will have the authority and the capacity to manage all activities occurring within some

---

[7] Although the caste system has no legal standing in the current Indian political order, it remains a significant force in everyday social relations.

spatially delimited boundaries will be untenable as a constitutive principle of such an order. Even today, the image of states as hard-shelled units that are able to manage their internal affairs without interference on the part of outsiders is little more than a convenient fiction. The growth of advanced technologies, including artificial intelligence, machine learning, and the Internet of Things, ensures that a range of actors will be able to penetrate each other's jurisdictional domains with relative ease. States already make use of these technologies to pursue worthy objectives like disseminating factual information on matters of common concern as well as antisocial objectives like using malware to disrupt or contaminate the operation of political systems in other states. But the growing influence of largely virtual actors whose operations pay little attention to traditional jurisdictional boundaries is creating a situation in which conventional thinking about internal sovereignty is less and less helpful as a guide to thinking about political order.

This means that the global political order of the future cannot be purely place-based in the sense that it features a system of territorially defined units that can and do exercise authority effectively within spatially delimited jurisdictional boundaries. Is there an alternative approach to jurisdiction that may replace the principle of internal sovereignty in a future order? The answer to this question is anything but clear at this stage. One response worth exploring centers on the idea that some polycentric system of functionally delimited authority may work better in a future global political order than the system of spatially defined authority that is a constitutive feature of the current order (Haas 1958; Lindberg and Scheingold 1970; Thiel et al. 2019). But this assumes that it would be feasible to devise workable distinctions among different functional domains (e.g. health, commerce, environmental protection) under conditions likely to prevail in the future. In a world featuring tight connections among a wide range of economic and social concerns, including major teleconnections, functionally delimited authority may not provide a workable alternative to spatially defined authority. Finding a suitable approach to the allocation of authority, not to mention creating effective procedures for resolving disputes about the application of any alternative principle of allocation to concrete situations, will emerge as one of the core concerns confronting those seeking to devise a political order capable of replacing the state-based system.

Predictably, some observers will fall back on the conclusion that there is no way to come to terms with the problems of the foreseeable future without creating some sort of world government. But this familiar prescription has well-known drawbacks that will not go away during the foreseeable future. Even in the unlikely event that we were to succeed in hammering out the terms of a global compact calling for the establishment of some sort of world government on paper, there is no basis for assuming that such a government would be able to exercise its authority effectively to make collective choices about matters of common concern, much less to mobilize and deploy the resources needed to implement these choices effectively. The efforts of such a government to steer human activities in a global setting containing eight to ten billion people having little in common and subject to intense polarizing forces might well give rise to authoritarian leadership pursuing illiberal goals and resorting to more-or-less harsh forms of repression in an effort to maintain control.

Is there an alternative way of managing the affairs of a system in which a diverse collection of actors seek to promote their own interests with limited concern for the impacts of their actions on others but in which tight telecoupling ensures that their actions have far-reaching consequences for the welfare of others in distant locations? It would be naive to assume that we will succeed under the conditions prevailing today in finding a workable solution to this challenge. It is apparent that some large political orders of the past have collapsed under the weight of internal contradictions they were unable to resolve. This could be the fate of a successor to the current order. Nevertheless, it would be inappropriate to conclude that there is no way out of this dilemma under conditions likely to prevail during the foreseeable future. Recent scholarship suggests that relatively large and diverse groups of humans have been able in some settings to manage their common affairs in the absence of an overarching government, even in the absence of modern technologies that make communication easy and inexpensive (Graeber and Wengrow 2021). In this regard, it will be interesting to explore opportunities afforded by the growth and diffusion of advanced technologies to elicit input regarding matters of common concern from very large numbers of people in a manner that is quick and cost-effective.

7.5 Addressing the Grand Challenges

Where does this discussion of the global political order of the future leave us in terms of finding ways to address the grand challenges of the twenty-first century? All these challenges are difficult – perhaps impossible – to address effectively within the confines of the state-based system. There are good reasons to conclude that coming to terms with climate change requires a fundamental transition away from efforts to maximize economic growth measured in material terms, a transition that cannot be brought about through the negotiation of international legally binding instruments like the UNFCCC and its various supplements (Skidelsky and Skidelsky 2012; Pilling 2018). Dealing with the spread of infectious diseases like COVID-19 calls for actors to join forces to engage in cooperative responses rather than blaming each other for specific outbreaks and turning inward in an attempt to shut themselves off from the impacts of diseases spreading elsewhere (Gates 2022). States seeking to deploy digital technologies as instruments in their efforts to gain the upper hand in the realm of geopolitics are part of the problem rather than part of the solution. The revolution in biotechnology is driven by forces that states seldom consider explicitly, let alone seek to steer in constructive ways.

It is impossible to assess whether a future global political order would provide effective means for coming to terms with these grand challenges in the absence of more details regarding the constitutive features of such an order. Nevertheless, several initial observations are in order at this stage. Implicit in mainstream thinking about a state-based system is a presumption that individual states will seek to maximize their relative power in interactions with one another, regardless of the consequences measured in terms of various conceptions of the common good (Waltz 1979). This is why many see the operation of a balance of power as a necessary condition for maintaining the resilience of the current order. But the resultant dynamic amounts to a fundamental obstacle when it comes to addressing the grand challenges of the twenty-first century. This suggests that we should direct attention to the extent to which this fixation with maximizing relative power can be subordinated to other drivers of behavior in any future global political order. The good news is that this is not a hopeless quest. While some see the fixation on relative power as an ineradicable feature of human nature, there are good reasons to conclude that this Hobbesian view of the human condition is a product of western civilization rather than an innate feature of human nature. Moving beyond a society dominated by power-maximizing states might allow us to promote the development of a society foregrounding some other driving forces.

If a future political order encompasses a mix of different types of actors, a critical issue will center on the extent to which cooperation, or at least coordination, between or among diverse actors becomes a normal practice. In the state-based system today, there is much talk about the potential of public–private partnerships. This is a significant development (Andonova et al. 2022). But such discussions generally reflect the assumption that authority still resides with states which may or may not choose to cooperate with nonstate actors on terms of their own devising (Milner and Moravcsik 2009). In a future global political order, there would be no presumption that actors similar to today's states are the sole repositories of political authority. It might take some time to sort out the rules of engagement among different types of actors in such a setting. The outcome might differ substantially from mainstream models based on western thinking about the rule of law. But this is not to say that chaos would ensue. It is perfectly possible that the breakdown of an entrenched system dominated by power-maximizing states more concerned with their place in the geopolitical standings than with addressing the grand challenges of planetary governance would open up opportunities to explore innovative responses to these concerns. At a minimum, it would reduce the influence of path dependence, which constitutes a major obstacle to introducing innovative approaches to systemic issues in all societies, including the state-based system as we know it today.

8 Pathways to a New Order

What are the options available to those convinced by my argument that it is difficult – perhaps impossible – to address the twenty-first century's grand challenges of planetary governance within the framework of the prevailing global order and looking for constructive responses to this dilemma? As I have noted, the behavior of complex systems involves interactions among numerous variables that ensure the frequency of surprises and make it hard to formulate policy recommendations with any confidence. Even so, some observations about pathways to a new order are worth considering.

It is helpful to draw a distinction between two broad classes of responses. One class, which we can think of as reformist, focuses on ways to adjust the current order to improve the results of efforts to meet needs for governance without triggering an immediate transition to some alternative form of political order, though the adjustments may lead to a transformation over the long run. This is the focus of those who draw attention to the idea of resilience and look for institutional adaptations within the framework of the prevailing order that seem both politically feasible and likely to enhance the capacity of a reformed order to come to terms with the grand challenges. The other class of responses includes options that are transformative even in the short run. These responses direct attention to innovations calling for fundamental changes in one or more of the constitutive features of the current order in the interests of devising effective ways to address the grand challenges of planetary governance.

8.1 Reformism

It seems accurate to say that reformism provides the first line of defense among most of those concerned with addressing issues of governance on a global scale. Among the main targets of reformers are adjustments in the precept of external sovereignty and the principle of internal sovereignty. Those who have developed our understanding of the current order as a state-based system often assert that sovereignty is indivisible. States are either sovereign or they are not; there is no middle ground. But this argument is not persuasive. Political orders are social constructs. They are products of human actions that are subject to change as a result of shifting perceptions, preferences, and practices. In this context, the principal target of the reformers centers on the effort to adjust our common understanding of sovereignty in such a way as to address major needs for governance arising on a global scale, without introducing fundamental changes in the constitutive provisions of the prevailing order.

Perhaps the most prominent example of reformism in modern times centers on the creation of the United Nations in 1945 as a means of preventing recurrent outbreaks of world war likely to lead to the demise of the state-based system. The Charter reaffirms the general idea of sovereignty as a key feature of the political order. But it imposes limitations on the freedom of states to act as they see fit with regard to "threats to the peace, breaches of the peace, and acts of aggression," and it endows the Security Council with the authority to make authoritative decisions regarding such matters in accordance with specific procedures set forth in Chapter VII. It is worth emphasizing in this regard that we have not witnessed the outbreak of a third world war and that classic interstate wars have declined in frequency during the decades following the creation of the United Nations, though this has not eliminated civil wars and many other types of organized political violence. This is good news from the point of view of coming to terms with a problem that has threatened to trigger a critical transition in the state-based system. But it would be difficult to make a convincing case that this development is attributable to the activities of the United Nations. Among other things, disagreements among the permanent members have regularly produced stalemate in efforts to make use of the authority of the Security Council to address disruptive situations, including the current military hostilities in Ukraine. It is important to note as well that conditions prevailing today offer no guarantee against the outbreak of wars involving the use of weapons of mass destruction in the future.

Another major focus of attention on the part of reformers centers on the protection of human rights. The critical issue here concerns the imposition of restrictions on the internal sovereignty of states with regard to their treatment of all those subject to their jurisdiction (Forsythe 2017). Arguably, the most prominent initiative in this context encompasses the adoption in 1948 of the Universal Declaration of Human Rights in the form of a UN General Assembly Resolution together with the subsequent effort to transform these rights in the form of the legally binding International Covenant on Civil and Political Rights and International Covenant on Economic, Social and Cultural Rights, both adopted in 1966. What has evolved in the intervening years is one of the major political battlegrounds in the state-based system, with reformers engaging in a longstanding campaign to strengthen human rights and the authorities of major states continuing to assert their sovereign authority to deal with human activities within their jurisdictions as they see fit. At this stage, it would be hard to make a convincing case that the reformers are gaining the upper hand in their campaign to impose restrictions on internal sovereignty in the name of protecting human rights. But there is no reason to expect the reformers to give ground with regard to their continuing efforts to protect human rights.

A third focus of reformers centers on the effort to hold political leaders accountable for what have been treated in the post-WWII era as crimes against humanity (Sands 2016). Starting with ad hoc initiatives including the International Criminal Tribunal for the Former Yugoslavia and the International Criminal Tribunal for Rwanda, this effort gained momentum with the adoption in 1998 of the Rome Statute creating the International Criminal Court (ICC) as an ongoing forum for addressing such crimes. Based in the Hague, the ICC has worked hard to bring individual leaders accused of committing a range of crimes against humanity within their own jurisdictions to justice. The Court has achieved successes in some specific instances. But major states (e.g. the United States) have refused to sign on to the Rome Statute, and the ICC has been unable to gain traction regarding a wide range of cases involving the sorts of crimes listed in the Statute. The campaign to address crimes against humanity is likely to continue indefinitely. So far, however, there is no basis for arguing that this campaign has produced a significant adjustment in the principle of internal sovereignty.

Whatever the fate of these reforms, is it realistic to expect that we can find ways to reform the prevailing order order to address the twenty-first century's grand challenges of global governance? There is no simple answer to this question. Without doubt, reformers will continue to make a determined effort to respond to these challenges without triggering a critical transition in the state-based system. Initiatives aimed at strengthening the climate regime based on the framework set forth in the UNFCCC and at negotiating a "pandemic treaty" as a key element in a strategy to deal with infectious diseases are cases in point (Phelan and Carlson 2022). These efforts may produce some positive results. But as the analysis presented in this Element makes clear, there are good reasons to be skeptical about the prospects that reform measures will prove sufficient to address the grand challenges effect-ively. This is not a reason to abandon the pursuit of reformist initiatives aimed at responding to the grand challenges. But it does suggest that it is important to add a sustained exploration of transformative changes in the prevailing order to the ongoing efforts of the reformers.

8.2 Transformationism

No political order lasts forever; there is every reason to expect that a critical transition leading to the demise of the current global order and the rise of some new political order will occur at some time. Yet the dynamics of complex systems ensure that we cannot make confident predictions regarding either the precise timing or the specific character of such a transition. Whether we are looking at physical systems such as the Earth's climate system or at social systems such as the current global political order, critical transitions virtually always have an element of surprise. There exists today a robust cottage industry populated by policy analysts seeking to make more or less explicit projections about the future of sovereign states and the future of the prevailing global order more generally. But there is no reason to take any of these projections seriously. Surprise is the norm when it comes to critical transitions in complex systems.

All this may seem disconcerting to those who are dedicated to the perpetuation of the state-based system as we know it today and who are, as a result, motivated to devise strategies intended to shore up this political order in the face various threats. But for others, the prospect that the future may bring a critical transition in the character of the global political order will seem more like an opportunity to embrace institutional innovation than a catastrophe to be avoided at all costs. Although both the onset and the trajectory of such a transition are difficult to anticipate, the conditions of crisis generated by the cascading changes associated with a critical transition often open up a window of opportunity to introduce far-reaching changes in institutional arrangements that seem solidly entrenched and immune to major adjustments during normal times. Whereas reaching agreement on specific adjustments in arrangements like those that make up the climate regime feels like pulling teeth under the conditions prevailing today, introducing fundamentally different strategies for addressing an issue like climate change may become feasible in the context of a critical transition.

In most cases, such windows do not remain open for long. This suggests a need to be prepared to respond vigorously in introducing innovative arrangements when the opportunity arises. Given the element of surprise in critical transitions, it is unrealistic to think that we can devise a detailed blueprint in advance setting forth the specific steps to be taken in the event of the onset of a critical transition in the state-based system. Nevertheless, we can engage in serious and sustained debate regarding the relative merits of alternative political orders that may become feasible as successors to the state-based system as we know it today. Proceeding in this way will not reduce the element of surprise associated with the occurrence of a critical transition in this order when it does occur. But it will strengthen our ability to respond in a vigorous and coherent manner when an opportunity arises to make substantial changes in the character of the global political order that has prevailed during the final decades of the twentieth century and the early decades of the twenty-first century.

Perhaps the most important issue to consider in this context centers on what I have described as the effects of scale. It seems unreasonable to expect that a successor to the current political order would feature a central or overarching government in the ordinary sense of the term. The diversity among human communities is too great to allow for effective governance under the terms of single constellation of institutions, much less a centralized political system. It is likely that a world government would be crippled by political dissension or bureaucratic paralysis. The prospect that any such arrangement might be captured by authoritarian leaders or rogue actors not committed to the common good is daunting. Under the circumstances, it makes sense to focus on arrangements featuring multilevel governance systems and to draw a clear distinction between policymaking and implementation in thinking about the global political order of the future. What this means is that it would be desirable to limit the authority of global institutions strictly to responding to those needs for governance that cannot be addressed at lower levels and to rely on lower levels to take responsibility for the implementation of policies adopted through the operation of global institutions (Raskin 2021). There is no guarantee that an effort to establish highly constrained global institutions along these lines would prove successful. Among other things, it seems unrealistic to expect that spontaneous processes would prove sufficient to deal with issues of coordination of the various elements of such an order (Ostrom 2010; Aligica and Tarko 2012). But innovation involving complex systems of this sort is what is needed in the realm of global political order.

There are some indications that the rise of digital technologies and the growing role of virtual reality may prove helpful in this regard. The governance of the Internet at least in its initial stages and the development of wikipedia have featured coordination systems involving a minimum of centralized authority (Brousseau et al. 2012). The dramatic growth of social media opens up the prospect of being able to consult huge numbers of people in real time regarding matters of common concern. Obviously, these are somewhat limited cases (Berners-Lee 2019; West and Allen 2020). They do not offer a blueprint for coming to terms with the twenty-first century's grand challenges of planetary governance. But they do suggest that we are entering a new era in which there is a growing need to engage in innovative thinking about approaches to governance made possible by the rise of digital technologies (Centola 2018).

Are these comments about the prospects for transformation in the global political order sufficient to engender a sense of optimism, or even confidence, regarding the development of strategies to address the grand challenges of planetary governance during the foreseeable future? There is no basis at this stage for answering this question affirmatively. Failures in efforts to address needs for governance at all levels of social organization are common. But these observations do offer an alternative to mainstream reformist strategies focusing on relatively limited adjustments that do not envision fundamental changes in the constitutive features of the current political order. Given the urgency of the issues associated with the grand challenges, the bottom line for me is that we need to make a sustained effort not only to pursue reformist strategies but also and especially to explore fundamental alternatives to the prevailing global order at the same time.

For those interested in transformationism, what are the next steps? I do not think it is possible to engineer the occurrence of a critical transition in the prevailing global political order. More often than not, we are taken by surprise when an event of this nature occurs, even though it may be apparent that the existing order features a variety of forces that are eroding its adaptive capacity. Nevertheless, I see two fruitful lines of enquiry arising from the analysis I have presented in this Element. One centers on delving deeper into what I have called constitutive pressures, systemic forces, and political tipping elements. How serious are the pressures on the dominant place of states in the current order arising from the growing influence of various types of nonstate actors? Am I right in arguing that the rise of virtual reality is eroding a political order highlighting the role of place-based actors? How can we adapt our thinking about tipping elements, developed by those interested in biophysical systems, to apply this set of ideas to understanding the dynamics of political orders? Answers to questions of this sort can help us to deepen our understanding of critical transitions in social systems, even if they are not likely to allow us to make confident predictions about the timing and the character of a critical transition in the current global political order in the coming years.

The other theme that comes into focus for those interested in transformation has to do with the institutional character of the global political order of the future. Critical transitions are apt to generate a sense of turmoil, at least in their earlier stages. But they are also turning points in the sense that arrangements that once seemed impervious to change are swept away, opening up opportunities to create new arrangements that differ in major ways from their predecessors. Here, too, a note of caution is in order. It would be a mistake to exaggerate the potential for social engineering in this realm. It is hard to anticipate how specific arrangements will operate in a complex system, much less to hammer out consensus among major actors regarding the constitutive features of a new order. Still, as the cases of the negotiation of the Constitution of the United States in 1987 and the formulation of the provisions of the Charter of the United Nations in 1944–5 make clear, constitutive moments do arise from time to time in human affairs.

What are the key questions that would deserve attention should such an opportunity arise on a global scale? Here are some examples. How should we think about the roles of states and nonstate actors in a new order? How can we bring to bear the concepts of polycentric governance and multi-level governance to allocate roles among distinct actors ranging from the local to the global and to ensure effective cross-level coordination? How can we manage interactions between physical reality and virtual reality in a future global order? What principles should govern interactions between human systems and biophysical systems, such as the Earth's climate system? There is ample scope for debate regarding answers to these and a stream of related questions. None of them has a correct answer in the sense of a response that can be counted on to produce the intended results. Even so, there is much to be said for thinking hard about the pros and cons of a range of options in the interests of making informed choices if and when a constitutive moment arises with regard to the global political order.

References

Acharaya, Amitav 2018 *The End of the American World Order*. 2nd ed. Cambridge: Polity Press.

Aligica, Paul D. and Vlad Tarko 2012 "Polycentricity: From Polanyi to Ostrom, and Beyond," *Governance: An International Journal of Policy, Administration, and Institutions*, 25: 237–262.

Allison, Graham 2017 *Destined for War: Can America and China Escape Thucydides's Trap*. New York: Houghton Mifflin.

Andonova, Liliana 2017 *Governance Entrepreneurs: International Organizations and the Rise of Public-Private Partnerships*. Cambridge, MA: MIT Press.

Andonova, Liliana B., Moira V. Faul, and Dario Piselli eds. 2022 *Partnerships for Sustainability in Contemporary Global Governance: Pathways to Effectiveness*. London: Routledge.

Bell, Duncan ed. 2008 *Victorian Visions of Global Order: Empire and International Relations in Nineteenth Century Political Thought*. Cambridge: Cambridge University Press.

Berners-Lee, Mike 2019 *There is No Planet B: A Handbook for the Make or Break Years*. Cambridge: Cambridge University Press.

Biermann, Frank 2014 *Earth System Governance: World Politics in the Anthropocene*. Cambridge, MA: MIT Press.

Biermann, Frank and Rakhyun E. Kim eds. 2020 *Architectures of Earth System Governance: Institutional Complexity and Structural Transformation*. Cambridge: Cambridge University Press.

Brousseau, Eric, Meryem Marzouki, and Cecile Meadel eds. 2012 *Governance, Regulations and Powers on the Internet*. Cambridge: Cambridge University Press.

Bull, Hedley 1977 *The Anarchical Society*. New York: Columbia University Press.

Centola, Damon 2018 *How Behavior Spreads: The Science of Complex Contagion*. Princeton, NJ: Princeton University Press.

Chayes, Abram and Antonia Handler Chayes 1995 *The New Sovereignty: Compliance with International Regulatory Agreements*. Cambridge, MA: Harvard University Press.

Clark, Granville and Louis B. Sohn 1962 *World Peace through World Law*. 2nd ed. Cambridge, MA: Harvard University Press.

Claude, Inis L. Jr. 1959 *Swords into Plowshares*. 2nd ed. New York: Random House.

Claude, Inis L. Jr. 1962 *Power and International Relations*. New York: Random House.

Coiffier, Jean 2012 *Fundamentals of Numerical Weather Prediction*. Cambridge: Cambridge University Press.

Cox, Robert W. 1987 *Production, Power, and World Order: Social Forces in the Making of History*. New York: Columbia University Press.

Crawford, Kate 2021 *Atlas of AI: Power, Politics, and the Planetary Costs of Artificial Intelligence*. New Haven, CT: Yale University Press.

Cueto, Marcus, Theodore M. Brown, and Elizabeth Fee 2019 *The World Health Organization: A History*. Cambridge: Cambridge University Press.

Dalio, Ray 2021 *Principles for Dealing with the Changing World Order*. New York: Avid Reader Press.

Dauvergne, Peter 2020 *AI in the Wild: Sustainability in the Age of Artificial Intelligence*. Cambridge, MA: MIT Press.

Davies, Kevin 2020 *Editing Humanity: The CRISPR Revolution and the New Era of Genome Editing*. New York: Pegasus Books.

DeNardis, Laura 2014 *The Global War for Internet Governance*. New Haven, CT: Yale University Press.

DeNardis, Laura 2020 *The Internet of Everything: Freedom and Security in a World with No Off Switch*. New Haven, CT: Yale University Press.

Dietz, Tom, Elinor Ostrom, and Paul C. Stern 2003 "The Struggle to Govern the Commons," *Science*, 302: 1907–1912.

Duit, Andreas and Victor Galaz 2008 "Governance and Complexity – Emerging Issues for Governance Theory,"*Governance: An International Journal of Policy, Administration and Institutions*, 21: 311–335.

Earth System Governance Project 2018 *Earth System Governance: Science and Implementation Plan of the Earth System Governance Project*. Utrecht: ESG.

Evans, John H. 2020 *The Human Gene Editing Debate*. Oxford: Oxford University Press.

Folke, Carl 2006 "Resilience: The Emergence of a Perspective for Social-Ecological Systems Analysis," *Global Environmental Change*, 16: 268–281.

Forsythe, David P. 2017 *Human Rights in International Relations*. Cambridge: Cambridge University Press.

Galaz, Victor 2014 *Global Environmental Governance, Technology and Politics: The Anthropocene Gap*. Cheltenham: Edward Elgar.

Gates, Bill 2022 *How to Prevent the Next Pandemic*. New York: Knopf.

Gibson, Clark, Elinor Ostrom, and Toh-Kyeong Ahn 2000 "The Concept of Scale and the Human Dimensions of Global Change: A Survey," *Ecological Economics*, 32: 217–239.

Gladwell, Malcom 2002 *Tipping Point: How Little Things Can Make a Big Difference*. New York: Little, Brown.

Godwin, William 2013 *An Enquiry Concerning Political Justice*. Oxford: Oxford University Press.

Graeber, David and David Wengrow 2021 *The Dawn of Everything: A New History of Humanity*. New York: Farrar, Straus, and Giroux.

Gunderson, Lance H. and Crawford S.Holling eds. 2002 *Panarchy: Understanding Transformations in Human and Natural Systems*. Washington, DC: Island Press.

Haas, Ernst B. 1958 *The Uniting of Europe: Political, Social, and Economic Forces, 1950–1957*. Stanford, CA: Stanford University Press.

Hall, Rodney Bruce and Thomas J. Biersteker eds. 2002 *The Emergence of Private Authority in Global Governance*. Cambridge: Cambridge University Press.

Harrison, Neil E. ed. 2007 *Complexity in World Politics: Concepts and Methods of a New Paradigm*. Albany, NY: State University of New York Press.

Hayek, Friedrich A. 1944 *The Road to Serfdom*. Chicago, IL: University of Chicago Press.

Hayek, Friedrich A. 1973 *Rules and Order*. Vol. 1 of *Law, Legislation, and Liberty*. Chicago, IL: University of Chicago Press.

Herz, John H. 1976 *The Nation-State and the Crisis of World Politics*. New York: David McKay.

Higgins, Eliot 2021 *We Are Bellingcat: Global Crime, Online Sleuths, and the Bold Future of News*. New York: Bloomsbury.

Hoffmann, Stanley 1966 "Obstinate or Obsolete? The Fate of the Nation-State and the Case of Western Europe," *Daedalus*, 95: 862–915.

Hurrell, Andrew 2007 *On Global Order: Power, Values, and the Constitution of International Society*. Oxford: Oxford University Press.

Isaacson, Walter 2014 *The Innovators: How a Group of Hackers, Geniuses, and Geeks Created the Digital Revolution*. New York: Simon and Schuster.

Isaacson, Walter 2021 *The Code Breaker: Jennifer Doudna, Gene Editing, and the Future of the Human Race*. New York: Simon and Schuster.

Janssen, Marco. ed. 2002 *Complexity and Ecosystem Management: The Theory and Practice of Multi-Agent Systems*. Cheltenham: Edward Elgar.

Jervis, Robert 1997 *System Effects: Complexity in Political and Social Life*. Princeton, NJ: Princeton University Press.

Johnson, Neil 2009 *Simply Complexity: A Clear Guide to Complexity Theory*. Oxford: Oneworld.

Jones, Dan 2021 *Powers and Thrones: A New History of the Middle Ages*. New York: Viking.

Kahl, Colin and Thomas Wright 2021 *Aftershock: Pandemic Politics and the End of the Old International Order*. New York: St. Martin's Press.

Kaldor, Mary 2003 *Global Civil Society: An Answer to War*. Cambridge: Polity Press.

Kaplan, Fred 2016 *Dark Territory: The Secret History of Cyber War*. New York: Simon and Schuster.

Kapsar, Kelley E., Ciara L. Hovis, Ramon FelipeBicudo da Silva et al. 2019 "Telecoupling Research: The First Five Years," *Sustainability*, 11: 1033. https://doi.org/10.3390/su11041033.

Kavalski, Emilian ed. 2015 *World Politics at the Edge of Chaos*. Albany, NY: State University of New York Press.

Kello, Lucas 2017 *The Virtual Weapon and International Order*. New Haven, CT: Yale University Press.

Keohane, Robert O. and Joseph S. Nye Jr. 1977 *Power and Interdependence: World Politics in Transition*. Boston, MA: Little, Brown.

Kissinger, Henry 2014 *World Order*. New York: Penguin Press.

Klimburg, Alexander 2017 *The Darkening Web: The War for Cyberspace*. New York: Penguin Press.

Kropotkin, Peter 2014 *Direct Struggle Against Capital: A Peter Kropotkin Anthology*. Oakland, CA: AK Press.

Lebow, Richard Ned 2018 *The Rise and Fall of Political Orders*. Cambridge: Cambridge University Press.

Lee, Kai-Fu 2021 *AI Superpowers: China, Silicon Valley, and the New World Order*. New York: Mariner Books.

Lee, Kai-Fu and Qiufan Chen 2021 *AI 2041: Ten Visions of Our Future*. New York: Currency.

Lenton, Timothy M. 2020 "Tipping Positive Change," *Philosophical Transactions of the Royal Society B*, 375: 1–8. https://doi.org/10.1098/rstb .2019.0123.

Lenton, Timothy M., Hermann Held, Elmar Kriegler et al. 2008 "Tipping Elements in the Earth's Climate System," *Proceedings of the National Academy of Sciences USA*, 105: 1786–1793.

Levin, Simon A. 1999 *Fragile Dominion – Complexity and the Commons*. Cambridge: Perseus.

Lindberg, Leon N. and Stuart A. Scheingold 1970 *Europe's Would-be Polity: Patterns of Change in the European Community*. Englewood Cliffs, NJ: Prentice-Hall.

Linklater, Andrew and Hidemi Suganami 2006 *The English School of International Relations: A Contemporary Reassessment*. Cambridge: Cambridge University Press.

Liu, Jianguo, Harold Mooney, Vanessa Hull et al. 2015 "Systems Integration for Global Sustainability," *Science*, 347: 963–974.

Liu, Jianguo, Vanessa Hull, Mateus Batistella et al. 2013 "Framing Sustainability in a Telecoupled World," *Ecology and Society*, 18(2): 26. https://www.jstor.org/stable/26269331.

Lyons, Gene M. and Michael Mastanduno eds. 1995 *Beyond Westphalia? State Sovereignty and International Intervention*. Baltimore, MD: Johns Hopkins University Press.

Mayewski, Paul A., Eelco E. Rohling, J. Curt Stager et al. 2004 "Holocene Climate Variability," *Quaternary Research*, 62: 243–255.

McKay, David Armstrong, Arie Staal, Jesse F. Abrams et al. 2022 "Updated Assessment Suggests >1.5°C Global Warming Could Trigger Multiple Climate Tipping Points," preprint of paper submitted to *Science*. https://doi .org/10.1002/essoar.10509769.1.

McNeill, Willam 1976 *Plagues and Peoples*. New York: Anchor Books.

Meadows, Donella H. 2008 *Thinking in Systems*. White River Junction, VT: Chelsea Green.

Metz, Cade 2021 *Genius Makers: The Mavericks Who Brought AI to Google, Facebook, and the World*. New York: Dutton.

Milner, Helen V. and Andrew Moravcsik eds. 2009 *Power, Interdependence, and Nonstate Actors in World Politics*. Princeton, NJ: Princeton University Press.

Mitchell, Melanie 2009 *Complexity: A Guided Tour*. Oxford: Oxford University Press.

Morris, Ian 2010 *Why the West Rules – For Now*. New York: Farrar, Straus, and Giroux.

Morrison, Charles E. 2022 "Reforming the Global Health Regime in Covid-19's Wake," *Global Asia*, 17(1): 36–45.

Nozick, Robert 1974 *Anarchy, State, and Utopia*. New York: Basic Books.

O'Connor, Timothy 2020 "Emergent Properties," *Stanford Encyclopedia of Philosophy*. http://seop.illc.uva.nl/entries/properties-emergent/.

Opello, Walter C. and Stephen J. Rosow 2004 *The Nation-State and Global Order*. 2nd ed. Boulder, CO: Lynne Rienner.

Orsini, Amandine, Philippe Le Prestre, Peter M. Haas et al. 2020 "Forum: Complex Systems and International Governance," *International Studies Review*, 22: 1008–1038.

Ostrom, Elinor 1990 *Governing the Commons: The Evolution of Institutions for Collective Action*. Cambridge: Cambridge University Press.

Ostrom, Elinor 2005 *Understanding Institutional Diversity*. Princeton, NJ: Princeton University Press.

Ostrom, Elinor 2010 "Beyond Markets and States: Polycentric Governance of Complex Economic Systems," *American Economic Review*, 100: 641–671.

Pearce, Fred 2007 *With Speed and Violence: Why Scientists Fear Tipping Points in Climate Change*. New York: Beacon Press.

Perlroth, Nicole 2020 *This Is How They Tell Me the World Ends: The Cyber-Weapons Arms Race*. New York: Bloomsbury.

Phelan, Alexandra L. and Colin J. Carlson 2022 "A Treaty to Break the Pandemic Cycle," *Science*, 377: 475–477.

Pilling, David 2018 *The Growth Delusion: Wealth, Poverty, and the Well-Being of Nations*. New York: Tim Duggan Books.

Proudhon, Pierre-Joseph 2011 *Property is Theft! A Pierre-Joseph Proudhon Reader*. Oakland, CA: AK Press.

Raskin, Paul 2021 *Journey to Earthland: The Great Transition to Planetary Civilization*. Cambridge, MA: Tellus Institute.

Raskin, Paul, Tariq Banuri, Gilberto Gallopín et al. 2002 *Great Transition: The Promise and Lure of the Times Ahead*. Boston, MA: Stockholm Environment Institute.

Reese, Byron 2018 *The Fourth Age: Smart Robots, Conscious Computers, and the Future of Humanity*. New York: Atria Books.

Robock, Alan 2010 "Nuclear Winter," *WIREs Climate Change*, 1(3): 418–427.

Rockström, Johan, Will Steffen, Kevin Noone et al. 2009 "A Safe Operating Space for Humanity," *Nature*, 461: 472–475.

Rodrik, Dani 2012 *The Globalization Paradox: Democracy and the Future of the World Economy*. New York: W. W. Norton.

Rosenau, James N. 1990 *Turbulence in World Politics*. Princeton, NJ: Princeton University Press.

Rosenau, James N. and Ernst-Otto Czempiel eds. 1992 *Governance without Government: Order and Change in World Politics*. Cambridge: Cambridge University Press.

Sachs, Jeffrey D. 2020 *The Ages of Globalization: Geography, Technology, and Institutions*. New York: Columbia University Press.

Sands, Philippe 2016 *East West Street: On the Origins of "Genocide" and "Crimes against Humanity."* New York: Knopf.

Scheffer, Marten 2009 *Critical Transitions in Nature and Society*. Princeton, NJ: Princeton University Press.

Scheffer, Marten, Stephen R.Carpenter, Timothy M. Lenton et al. 2012 "Anticipating Critical Transitions," *Science*, 338: 344–348.

Scott, James C. 2012 *Two Cheers for Anarchism: Six Pieces on Autonomy, Dignity, and Meaningful Work and Play*. Princeton, NJ: Princeton University Press.

Scott, James C. 2017 *Against the Grain: A Deep History of the Earliest States.* New Haven, CT: Yale University Press.

Sebenius, James K. 1984 *Negotiating the Law of the Sea.* Cambridge, MA: Harvard University Press.

Segal, Adam 2016 *The Hacked World Order: How Nations Fight, Trade, Maneuver, and Manipulate in the Digital Age.* New York: Public Affairs.

Skidelsky, Robert and Edward Skidelsky 2012 *How Much Is Enough? Money and the Good Life.* New York: Other Press.

Slaughter, Anne-Marie 2017 *The Chess-Board and the Web: Strategies of Connection in a Networked World.* New Haven, CT: Yale University Press.

Smith, Jackie, Charles Chatfield, and Ron Pagnucco eds. 1997 *Transnational Social Movements and Global Politics: Solidarity Beyond the State.* Syracuse, NY: Syracuse University Press.

Snowden, Frank 2019 *Epidemics and Society: From the Black Death to the Present.* New Haven, CT: Yale University Press.

Spengler, Oswald 2021 *The Decline of the West: Form and Actuality.* New York: Arktos Media.

Squatrito, Theresa, Oran R. Young, Andreas Follesdal, and Geir Ulfstein eds. 2018 *The Performance of International Courts and Tribunals.* Cambridge: Cambridge University Press.

Steffen, Will, Angelina Sanderson, Peter D. Tyson et al. 2004 *Global Change and the Earth System: A Planet under Pressure.* Berlin: Springer.

Steffen, Will, Katherine Richardson, Johan Rockström et al. 2015 "Planetary Boundaries: Guiding Human Development on a Changing Planet," *Science,* 347(6223): 1–11. https://doi.org/10.1126/science.1259855.

Stiglitz, Joseph E. 2003 *Globalization and Its Discontents.* New York: W. W. Norton.

Thiel, Andreas, William A. Blomquist, and Dustin E. Garrick eds. 2019 *Governing Complexity: Analyzing and Applying Polycentricity.* Cambridge: Cambridge University Press.

Toynbee, Arnold 1946 *A Study of History.* Oxford: Oxford University Press.

Tsebelis, George 2003 *Veto Players: How Political Institutions Work.* Princeton, NJ: Princeton University Press.

UDHR 1948 *Universal Declaration of Human Rights*, UN General Assembly Res. 217 A (III) of 10 December 1948. www.un.org/en/development/desa/popula tion/migration/generalassembly/docs/globalcompact/A_RES_217(III).pdf.

United Nations 1945 *United Nations Charter.* www.un.org/en/about-us/un-charter/full-text.

van der Leeuw, Sander and Carl Folke 2021 "The Social Dynamics of Basins of Attraction," *Ecology and Society*, 26(1): 33. https://doi.org/10.5751/ES-12289–260133.

Waddell, Steve and Sanjeev Khagram 2007 "Multi-stakeholder Global Networks: Emerging Systems for the Global Common Good," 261–287 in Pieter Glasbergen, Frank Biermann, and Arthur P. J. Mol eds. *Partnerships, Governance and Sustainable Development: Reflections on Theory and Practice*. Cheltenham: Edward Elgar.

Walker, Brian and David Salt 2006 *Resilience Thinking: Sustaining Ecosystems and People in a Changing World*. Washington, DC: Island Press.

Waltz, Kenneth 1979 *Theory of International Relations*. Reading, MA: Addison-Wesley.

Wang, Ban ed. 2017 *Chinese Visions of World Order*. Durham, NC: Duke University Press.

Webb, Amy and Andrew Hessel 2022 *The Genesis Machine: Our Quest to Rewrite Life in the Age of Synthetic Biology*. New York: Public Affairs.

Weber, Max (transl. Talcott Parsons) 1930 *The Protestant Ethic and the Spirit of Capitalism*. London: Unwin.

Wedgwood, Cicely V. 2005 *The Thirty Years' War*. New York: NYRB Classics.

West, Darrell M. and John R. Allen 2020 *Turning Point: Policymaking in the Era of Artificial Intelligence*. Washington, DC: Brookings Institution Press.

Young, Oran R. 1997 *Governance in World Affairs*. Ithaca, NY: Cornell University Press.

Young, Oran R. 2017 *Governing Complex Systems: Social Capital for the Anthropocene*. Cambridge, MA: MIT Press.

Young, Oran R. 2021 *Grand Challenges of Planetary Governance: Global Order in Turbulent Times*. Cheltenham: Edward Elgar.

Young, Oran R., Jian Yang, and Daniel J. Guttman 2020 "Meeting Cyber Age Needs for Governance in a Changing Global Order," *Sustainability*, 12 (5557): 1–17. https://doi.org/10.3390/su12145557.

Zhao, Tingyang 2019 *Redefining a Philosophy for World Governance*. Singapore: Palgrave Pivot.

About the Author

Oran Young has devoted his career to theoretical and applied research on the roles that social institutions play in addressing needs for governance in a variety of settings. His applied work deals with marine issues, atmospheric issues, the polar regions, and comparative studies of environmental governance in China and the United States.

Cambridge Elements ≡

Earth System Governance

Frank Biermann
Utrecht University

Frank Biermann is Research Professor of Global Sustainability Governance with the Copernicus Institute of Sustainable Development, Utrecht University, the Netherlands. He is the founding Chair of the Earth System Governance Project, a global transdisciplinary research network launched in 2009; and Editor-in-Chief of the new peer-reviewed journal *Earth System Governance* (Elsevier). In April 2018, he won a European Research Council Advanced Grant for a research program on the steering effects of the Sustainable Development Goals.

Aarti Gupta
Wageningen University

Aarti Gupta is Professor of Global Environmental Governance at Wageningen University, The Netherlands. She is Lead Faculty and a member of the Scientific Steering Committee of the Earth System Governance (ESG) Project and a Coordinating Lead Author of its 2018 Science and Implementation Plan. She is also principal investigator of the Dutch Research Council-funded TRANSGOV project on the Transformative Potential of Transparency in Climate Governance. She holds a PhD from Yale University in environmental studies.

Michael Mason
London School of Economics and Political Science (LSE)

Michael Mason is Associate Professor in the Department of Geography and Environment at the London School of Economics and Political Science (LSE). At LSE he also Director of the Middle East Centre and an Associate of the Grantham Institute on Climate Change and the Environment. Alongside his academic research on environmental politics and governance, he has advised various governments and international organisations on environmental policy issues, including the European Commission, ICRC, NATO, the UK Government (FCDO) and UNDP.

About the Series

Linked with the Earth System Governance Project, this exciting new series will provide concise but authoritative studies of the governance of complex socio-ecological systems, written by world-leading scholars. Highly interdisciplinary in scope, the series will address governance processes and institutions at all levels of decision-making, from local to global, within a planetary perspective that seeks to align current institutions and governance systems with the fundamental 21st Century challenges of global environmental change and earth system transformations.

Elements in this series will present cutting edge scientific research, while also seeking to contribute innovative transformative ideas towards better governance. A key aim of the series is to present policy-relevant research that is of interest to both academics and policy-makers working on earth system governance.

More information about the Earth System Governance project can be found at:
www.earthsystemgovernance.org

Cambridge Elements ≡

Earth System Governance

Elements in the Series

A full series listing is available at: www.cambridge.org/EESG

Printed in the United States
by Baker & Taylor Publisher Services